Embodied BUSINESS

A guide to grounding and aligning your
business chakras for empathpreneurs

Tara Jackson

ISBN:
978-1-913590-07-9 (Paperback)
978-1-913590-08-6 (ebook)

Chakra images designed by Ami Ellis, Spiky Design.
Cover design by Lynda Mangoro, Creative Genie.

The Unbound Press
www.theunboundpress.com

Hey unbound one!

Welcome to this magical book brought to you by The Unbound Press.

At The Unbound Press we believe that when women write freely from the fullest expression of who they are, it can't help but activate a feeling of deep connection and transformation in others. When we come together, we become more and we're changing the world, one book at a time!

This book has been carefully crafted by both the author and publisher with the intention of inspiring you to move ever more deeply into who you truly are.

We hope that this book helps you to connect with your Unbound Self and that you feel called to pass it on to others who want to live a more fully expressed life.

With much love,

Nicola Humber

Founder of The Unbound Press
www.theunboundpress.com

Reviews

A must read for anyone starting out on their spiritual business journey, Embodied Business is like having your own personal business coach. Tara shares her own business journey with heart, authenticity and transparency sharing both the ups and downs, the lessons and blessings that come with running your own business. While Tara's own story is so inspiring, she also steps back and offers prompts and exercises within each section of the book to empower the reader to work through their own mindset blocks and other challenges that come up as business owners. Although I have been running my own business for many years now, it was still so useful to work through these prompts and I had lots of ah hah moments and clarity around my business while reading. This is such a beautiful book and definitely one for the shelves of all empathpreneurs, spiritpreneurs and those looking to do their lightwork as a full time gig.
Vix Maxwell, soul reader, business mentor and author, www.newagehipster.co

I literally couldn't put Embodied Business down! Even though I've had my own business for over 10 years now, I received SO many insights and a-ha moments from reading this magical book. I've never thought about my business in relation to the chakra system before, but I certainly will do from now on. This feels like essential reading to any empathic entrepreneur. I can imagine myself using it as an oracle on a day-to-day basis. Thank you so much Tara for bringing through this system and writing this much-needed book!
Nicola Humber, author and unbound writing mentor, www.nicolahumber.com

Embodied Business is a magical and extremely timely guide! Tara underscores how the entrepreneurial journey is a wonderful opportunity for personal discovery, healing and growth. Through relatable and encouraging anecdotes from her own experience; journaling prompts; and practical action steps, Tara inspires you to connect with and trust in yourself and trust that you're divinely supported – in your business, and in your life as a whole. Her

book reminds us of the interconnectedness of all things. That how we show up, and the results we see – in business and in life – are intertwined in more ways than we may think. In this book, you're challenged to transcend what you've been taught to believe and embrace a new paradigm where we simultaneously honour ourselves, our work, each other and our beautiful home, this earth.
Lulu Kitololo, artist and designer, www.lulukitololo.com

As a sensitive business owner myself, it can be hard to understand what is and isn't yours to carry energetically. I have been tracking my own energy levels for some time knowing it is important to honour your sensitivity, but Tara's book is full of gold to really help you clear the blocks and anything that could be holding you back. If you are a sensitive business owner, this is THE book you need to remind you that the one thing that is consistent in your business is YOU.
Sarah Lloyd, PR alchemist, author and radio host, www.indigosoulpr.com

Embodied Business is the ultimate guide for sensitives who long to thrive in the business world. Tara bridges the gap so beautifully and this book is such a powerful tool in creating a business that is energetically sustainable and in alignment with the soul. Embodied Business is a long awaited celebration for all empaths and highly sensitives who are tired of sitting on the sidelines. With Tara's guidance the reader really does come to the realisation that sensitivity is a SUPERPOWER. I love the way Tara opens the space for every part of ourselves to be celebrated and how to come to the inner union of divine masculine and feminine. This book is an incredibly grounding tool for bringing those higher self ideas down into the body and then out into the world.
Julia Tobin, creative consultant, www.instagram.com/follow.your.glow

Tara offers we 'empath entrepreneurs' an intriguing new perspective on how to be in relationship with our business through understanding how the different chakras relate to both ourselves and to the work we are here to do. Not only that, she also provides us with practical examples and questions to consider, to begin to

incorporate this new way of thinking and – importantly – feeling into our businesses. Tara's ideas and approach were completely novel to me but I immediately resonated with them. I had several 'aha' moments as I considered where my blocks might be and I used her guidance to explore how I could move forward. I know this is a book I will return to again and again to support me as I continue my journey as an entrepreneur. Tara's writing style is like sitting down to coffee with a good friend: she shares generously, with sensitivity and clarity, and always with the reader's best interests at heart.
Anna Sansom, writer and desire line walker,
www.annasansom.com

Using her personal story coupled with her spiritual expertise understanding the body mind and soul with chakras, Tara invites us to take a deep dive into living life with purpose through our work. A good entrepreneur relies on standard practice. A great entrepreneur understands in the times we live in, more is required to make a true lasting impact with the business we choose to engage in. More importantly, self care and knowing oneself is paramount to leadership and in order to achieve business goals, your life goals must be in alignment, not in conflict. This books empowers us to be individuals connected to community and our environment to transform as we walk our professional paths. Highly recommend it if you want to keep taking what you do to the next level. Get ready to be uncomfortable, to take chances, be surprised, and to come out the other side better than before!
Ngosa Chungu, Ndhlovukhazi storyteller,
www.twitter.com/whoops_c

As an empath in business I found this book to be a rich source of information. It's beautifully written and by breaking it down into the chakras it makes it easy to tackle the different areas of ourselves in business. Great check-in book which I will refer to often.
Meron Shapland, CBT/EFT therapist,
www.soulscapeyourlife.com

Contents

Introduction and how to use this book

Welcome,

It is an honour to have you here.

I have written this book for empaths on the entrepreneurial journey, particularly those newer to it or just starting out. I feel that we are told so much about business and what to do to succeed in it from the left brain perspective (which is the more logical, analytical and rational side; so could translate into things like systems and processes, for example), but less about what might come up on the entrepreneurial, inner energetic journey. Some of the things that affect how you might show up; that block you from sharing; that prevent you from taking aligned action; or that will support you to be the most you can be on this path. I find these areas can link to the seven main chakras in your body and I will share how they connect as we go on. These areas have been the biggest growth lessons for me personally and have made my entrepreneur journey even more rewarding and fulfilling.

It is my intention in this book to present some of the things that showed up for me, along with some suggestions for how to work with them and support yourself to move through them.

The book is split into a few sections. The first section is an overview of my entrepreneurial journey. I share it to illustrate where I am coming from and how this journey has unfolded for me. When I first began as an entrepreneur I would have liked to know more about others on this path as it felt quite lonely and I didn't know many others on this journey. So I share some of mine (and continue to throughout the book) in case you might be looking for the same. I then share an introduction and a bit about what you can expect in this book.

After that, it is the chakras section. There I cover the seven main chakras in the body and the two anchoring chakras of the soul star and the earth star as points above and below for love, grounding, nourishment, and connection.

For each chakra in the body, I go into more depth on the things that might come up that could hold you back from showing up as you are here to do. I include many stories from my own experience, stories from clients, insights, suggestions, inspiration, prompts, and tips for you to dive deeper into how it relates to you. Some may resonate with you, others may not.

You might like to start with one chakra and work your way into the others (as they apply to you). You might alternatively like to pick a page at random and work through it that way. You may find that you come back and re-visit chakras again and again as you go into deeper levels of awareness, growth and expansion. There is no right or wrong way to do this. It is about trusting what feels good to you. The one thing I do recommend is that you take the time to do the practical exercises in the areas that resonate, after all this is how change will happen for you.

All of the chakras are interconnected and overlap with one another. What comes up as a block in one may resonate more in another and I really recommend that you do what feels right for you. I will say that if you come across areas where there is resistance or you feel you might need to go deeper into possibly traumatic experiences, please, please reach out for support from someone you trust. I can also support you here and there are details in the resources section at the end about how to book a free session for us to get to know one another and feel into what it might be like to work together.

The earth star and soul star chakras include my tips for creating a business that nourishes you and remind you of the support available to you from above and below. Wellbeing is essential to the entrepreneurial journey and a huge part of the work I do. I know, for you to do the work you are here to do, you have to prioritise your wellness, and for your work to be nourishing and sustainable, your wellbeing is non-negotiable.

At the end of this book, there is a resources section with a simple guide to holistic wellness for each chakra (should you want to explore further), plus some additional ways to go deeper and resources to support you.

I hope this book supports you to align and ground your business and get to the bottom of any inner blocks that might be holding you back, so that you can shine and share your gifts which are so needed at this time.

Tara x

A letter to empathpreneurs

You are here for a purpose. Your soul carries the wisdom and knowledge of many lifetimes and places. You know it in your heart.

I know how hard it can be living in this world that doesn't fully honour sensitivity and compassion. I know how hard it can be to see and feel all the struggles and destruction. It's heartbreaking and can seem like too much.

Now is not the time to shy away. Now is the time to take a stand for what you believe in. Now is the time to let your love, compassion, and sensitivity lead. Now is the time to speak up.

You must prioritise your wellbeing; it's an essential part of your mission as an empathpreneur. You need to look after yourself so radically, deeply and magically, to honour your needs so that you can be the most YOU possible, as you are so needed at this time.

Now is the time to come together. Let yourself be held and supported in your mission. Reach out as you need it. Work in partnership with others.

But above all, come back to yourself, your heart, all parts of your body, your wise inner knowing. For it is there that you'll find answers whenever you seek them.

Thank you for being you and for bringing your unique magic. Now is the time to shine, for the good of all, and you!

I honour you for being on this journey and for showing up.

A little bit about my entrepreneurial journey

My entrepreneurial journey began when I was nine years old, one summer, on a Greek island with my family. We had found a smaller beach with fewer tourists. The beach was covered in pumice stones – the ones that are great for getting rid of dead skin cells and buffing. So, along with my younger siblings, we collected as many of the stones as we could carry and took them back to the main beach where we sold them for a few drachmas each to tourists. We did this for a good part of the summer and made quite a bit of money, especially for those days!

As a child, I always found ways to make extra money in my school holidays. I'd collect all my old toys and books and sell them by the side of the road; I helped out in a café; I baked for cake sales; and I would offer to help people with tasks in exchange for pocket money. Even if there wasn't money involved, I'd find ways to be 'running my own business', one of which was playing 'offices' with my younger siblings (I really did rope them into my endeavours!) and having pretend meetings.

Years later, when I began working in an office after University, I knew that I was going to have my own business one day. My best friend, Lulu, (who also has the entrepreneurial gene) and I would have conversations about it together, neither of us knew what we'd each be doing, but we did know that it was going to happen. I'm so grateful I had that support and like-minded friend from the beginning.

Over the next ten years I did everything to learn as much as I could to help me figure out what I wanted to do and feel confident enough to have my own business. I began working for my cool older cousin in London who had a PR company, climbing up the career ladder to account manager level, but then deciding that was enough for me. I had got far enough and now needed to try something else. Then I became a PA and office/business manager so I could learn the ins and outs of a small business, working closely with the Directors. Within that role I got to manage and plan events as well as learn all about the behind the scenes parts of a business: from finances, HR, and business administration, to new business development and marketing. I am incredibly grateful for that experience as it taught me so much.

However, I got weary of being full-time and doing the same thing over and over for one company. In all honesty, I didn't like being told what to do all the time, so I bit the freelance bullet and went off on my own, taking the first tentative step in working for myself. I still didn't really know what I wanted to have my own business in, so freelancing was a good option: it meant I could use my experience to support others, pay the bills, and have a bit more control over who I worked for and what hours I worked.

The freelancing was definitely up and down, totally rewarding in terms of time for myself, but also super hard at times as it certainly wasn't consistent, and I had many months where I was struggling to pay rent. It was also quite lonely in the beginning as I didn't know many others on this path, and it was quite an adjustment from working in an office filled with people. But I knew it would all be worth it someday and the freedom I felt at being more in control of my own time far outweighed any salary I had ever received. During that time, I also got to work for a huge number of businesses that I believed in: a pioneer in ethical and sustainable hospitality, food businesses, coaches, an energy healer, an ethical café, and a number of charities.

I was getting closer to knowing what I wanted to have my own business in but knew I wanted it to also include personal growth and health as I had always devoured books on the subjects. I began studying nutrition and health and wellness coaching on the side with the Institute for Integrative Nutrition in New York and The School of Natural Health Sciences in the UK. These trainings also supported, and in many ways kick-started, my own healing journey, which included a lot of work around my own self-worth and issues from my past, which you can read about in my first book 'Embodied – A self-care guide for sensitive souls'.

I finally officially opened up my own health and wellness coaching business in January 2016. I knew I wanted to focus on workplace wellness, having come from that environment and recognising a real need for change there. At this point I was still doing a tiny bit of freelancing in business administration and PR but I was all ready to start coaching and working full-time for myself. I began by researching over 200 small businesses in London that I could target with my services and sent out a marketing email to each offering them a free lunchtime workshop. They could choose one on energy levels or stress management. I was quite excited to be doing my own thing at last but, after sending out that email, I heard nothing back from any of them apart from one which thanked me and said they'd keep my details on file. I know that getting no response is not uncommon, but it certainly threw me as I thought I had a really good offer – it was free, so who wouldn't want it? I had expected to be fully booked and quitting the last bit of freelance work I was doing by the end of the month. But it didn't happen that way for me. I also didn't want to follow up with a phone call, which I knew was needed. So I left my workshop idea and moved on to PR'ing myself with the media. This was an area that felt safe to me: I could sit behind my laptop and draft wellness articles in response to stories the media were writing, and not have to speak or be seen.

I knew I had underlying confidence issues around speaking and sharing what I was doing. Even the thought of running a workshop in person petrified me at the time. There was an inner conflict going on of wanting to have my own business but being in fear of what that actually meant and what I would have to do. So I kept doing what felt good and what I knew how to do, which was developing media relationships via email with a number of wellness outlets and writing and sending them posts and articles. As a result, I got featured in a large number of print and online media during this time.

I slowly began doing free one-to-one coaching to build up my confidence and started to get some incredible results with people. I also started offering free 30-day seasonal self-care challenges – which were what I felt I needed as I was still struggling to find a wellness balance (which I will share more about later). I had hundreds of people joining my self-care challenges. This was reassuring, but I also felt like such a fraud as I didn't feel like I had my health and wellness together at all. How could I be the one helping people in this area when my own health and wellness were still such a work in progress?

Meanwhile, in my personal life, my awakening journey had taken full hold. I felt all over the place: struggling to get my business off the ground; not looking after myself as well as I wanted to; feeling like there was something more to life, something deeper, but I wasn't sure what it was. I was voraciously searching for answers online, looking at what other entrepreneurs were doing, and trying to find something that resonated. I stumbled across Ebonie Allard's (a life coach) Instagram account and a post with a competition to win several prizes including a business tarot card reading with Vix Maxwell, also known as New Age Hipster, plus lots of other goodies including oracle cards and books from Hay House, a weekend workshop with Jamie Catto, a meditation lesson, an online course with Ebonie, and more. I entered it thinking it would be cool to get all that stuff, and I actually won it! The prizes were so incredible in starting me off on my spiritual journey but the one that stuck with me was the reading from Vix Maxwell. As part of my reading I had asked why I might be struggling with getting my business started as I had been at it for over a year. Vix suggested that I may have blocks coming up around money and that there may be underlying beliefs around what I thought a business should look like, and that these were areas I could look into. Although I didn't fully know what she meant at the time – having never heard of these things before – something clicked, and I knew that's what I had to do.

At that same time, a friend from work who was also into spirituality, recommended 'Light is the New Black' by Rebecca Campbell. This book literally changed my life as it reminded me of my deep knowing that we are spiritual beings. I felt like I was coming home to myself. From then on, I lapped up everything Rebecca Campbell had to offer. I did her course in running a business and won a one-to-one mentoring session with her. I also volunteered at her first big live event and there I met soul sisters who I went on to collaborate with and have as friends. One of these soul sisters, Julia, was integral to my entrepreneurial journey as we later supported one another on a weekly basis and she always encouraged me and believed in my vision.

The mentoring session with Rebecca, aside from being incredibly helpful and supportive, was a 'moment' which led me on to the next thing that supported me in my entrepreneurial journey. These 'moments' are the pivotal points where I've met someone or done something that has led me on to the next thing that I have needed on my journey. As these moments happened, I began to surrender to my journey, knowing that it was unfolding exactly as it was meant to.

Rebecca recommended a networking event in London for more soulful entrepreneurs, where you could share your business and meet likeminded others. Although I was totally nervous as I had hated networking when I worked in PR, I knew it felt right, and I signed up for the next one, which was a couple of months away.

It was here that I met my first mentor, and now a close friend, Lara, who helps people align with abundance and their purpose. We connected in one of the one-to-one networking sessions and, from the minute I met her, I knew I was going to work with her somehow and that she was a part of my soul journey. Lara really saw me and my fears around visibility without me even having to say anything. She saw how I could help people. And she saw the 'me' inside that I knew was in there but was so buried beneath all the layers of 'life' that I almost didn't know if she still existed. But she did. I signed up to work with Lara straight away and through that work, I began to peel away the layers. Layers that I didn't even know existed. Layers around being seen and speaking up and sharing as well as opening up to receiving.

As I began to unpick those layers I realised that business isn't just what I had been taught and what I had experienced so far, there was so much more to it energetically – your mindset, any subconscious beliefs you might have, whether you are aligned, your capacity to receive, and more. This made so much sense to me and this is where the real work began.

I began to dive into these areas in any way I could find support. When I do something, I immerse myself in it fully and this was no exception. I spent any money that wasn't going on my essentials, and used credit cards, an overdraft and loans, on courses around prosperity, manifesting, energy healing, inner child work, writing to heal yourself, worthiness, self-sabotage, body love, past lives, meditations, boundaries, and forgiveness. I also devoured anything free from Hay House, listening to their entire annual summit with over 100 speakers and doing almost all of the free exercises given by the speakers. I did many free meditation series by Deepak Chopra and Oprah, free online workshops, read so many books and blogs I have lost count, and more. I was fully seeking, wanting to know it all and how it could support me on my personal and entrepreneurial journey.

I may have opened up Pandora's box, but now that it was open I certainly wasn't going to stop. I love, love, love the journey of exploration and doing it on myself has been one of the most fulfilling experiences of my life. I began to trust myself and my inner guidance like never before, I remembered my inner strength, I let go and healed so much, and today I can fully feel the difference in myself.

I also began to feel more confident in how I supported clients and started to attract some awesome opportunities for myself, such as being recommended by one of the main magazines for PAs to be a speaker on wellness at the annual Office trade show in London.

This way of doing things certainly isn't for everyone, but one of the reasons I did it was so I could help others one day. Being aware of so many modalities and learning the multiple ways to approach the same thing fascinates me.

As I explored all of these different areas, and learned about the people sharing and working in them, I knew that I wanted to do the same. Around this time I was also learning about empaths and highly sensitive people, and I knew straight away that I was one. This changed something inside of me. Suddenly it meant it was okay to feel so much, that I wasn't overly sensitive and emotional, and that I wasn't alone in feeling the way I did. There were others like me. There was strength in being the way I was, and I knew that – having thought for so long that there was something wrong with me for being who I was – I wanted to work with other empathic, highly sensitive people. I intuitively started a Facebook group called 'Self-care for empaths' (which I have since archived) and in it began to share other empath's stories and offer self-care support.

Another pivotal moment for me was joining an online women's circle with women from all backgrounds and all over the world. This experience was profound for me in terms of being seen, it also connected me with my soul family, without which I wouldn't be where I am today. I had to speak up and share my voice each week and, in doing so, overcame my fears of what I thought others might think of me. I shared the most vulnerable moments of my life with women who didn't judge me; they only mirrored back love and understanding. I realised we are all more alike than we are different and I was able to heal. I learned to receive help and support without expectation or guilt. I share more about this experience, and how it supported me to work through some of the blocks that were coming up in me, later in the book.

But the biggest thing I gained was the incredible connections. I have received support and assistance that has kept me going, friends and soul family who cheered me on when I put something new out into the world, who listened when I had those days where I wanted to give up, some of whom I still am lucky enough to work with today. Through these incredible women I have met more incredible empaths and healers, people who want to make a difference in this world by helping others to be the best that they can, to care for this planet and to rise together.

During this time I found the confidence to write my first book and to start leading workshops around seasonal and cyclical living, self-love and self-care. I was supporting clients in these areas with great success – after a few months of working with me, they had changed and let go of so much. It finally started to feel like I was on the right track.

However, just as I started to feel that way, I hit a lull. My intuition was telling me that all of the wellness work in seasonal self-care and self-love I was doing was more for my own journey, than for sharing with others. It was there to pave the way for something else. Later I learned what that was: my work with empath entrepreneurs.

In creating 'Empathpreneurs®', my current business which supports empath entrepreneurs with the various sides of an online business, I had been in a space of seeming nothingness for about six months. I had my book out in the world and was sharing it as it wanted to be shared, but nothing else was coming intuitively for me and my business. My mind was getting super frustrated and wanting to do something, so I was creating offers that I knew weren't aligned and sharing them to no avail. Whenever I connected with my intuition, asking for guidance on my next step, I wouldn't receive anything. One time I felt a giant cocoon, as if what was coming was still metamorphosing. I began to trust this and allowed myself to melt into the space in between: trusting that something would come. It did. Like a tonne of bricks. In less than an hour at the end of January 2020 the idea for 'Empathpreneurs®' flooded out of me and combined all of my experiences and areas I'd worked in. It was such a magical experience and truly taught me the importance of trusting and allowing the process.

I know that my business, Empathpreneurs®, is here to support other empaths, sensitives, healers and lightworkers to bring their gifts into the world. The world needs the empaths and sensitive ones who care about this planet to step into their power and own their worth so we can help each other and care for this home of ours. We are here to create a new paradigm, a new way of living. To create heaven on earth.

Since that first download it has been easy to share Empathpreneurs® with others and it is simply flowing. This is so different to when I first started out and was trying to share my wellness coaching. I allow my business to tell me what it needs and I have aligned myself to this new way of working and doing business that I truly believe is life-changing and is a huge part of this new earth that we empathpreneurs are here to be a part of.

When I started Empathpreneurs®, I knew it wanted a book to be written with my experiences and some of the things I had learned to support other empaths in business. It had been less than a year since my last book, I was doing training to become a Colour Mirrors practitioner, and I wasn't sure I wanted to write another one so soon and while doing such in-depth training. But this book wanted to be birthed and it came flooding out in the space of three weeks, as I surrendered to it and let it guide me.

My entrepreneurial journey has not always been easy; I have shed layers of conditioning and beliefs. I have questioned why I am doing it, wondered whether I was right for it. I have struggled financially and have gone around in circles. But it has also led me on the most incredible journey of exploration, self-discovery, self-awareness and self-expansion. To come to a place where business is about balancing the heart with the mind. Where it needs the feminine balanced with the masculine. Where, when you honour the periods of rest and trust the timing of how things unfold, you will create something so much more aligned and magical than you could even imagine.

It is my mission to support you in realising this for yourself so that you too can remember how supported you are and that you are here for a reason.

Empathpreneurs® – aligning your business with the chakras

When the idea first came to me to relate each chakra to a part of your business, I couldn't believe how perfectly everything I had been doing in my working life so far, and that I wanted to do to serve others (all of the freelance work and business work I was doing, combined with the wellness, self-love and spirituality), fitted together and could be linked to each chakra.

It was like I had been working towards this for the past 20 years. You really can't make it up and it just shows you how things come together in their own timing.

It first came as the more practical sides of your business, which linked as follows:

- Base Chakra: your business basics: your website presence, social media profiles, accounting, invoicing and other systems and processes.
- Sacral Chakra: your brand and identity: your unique brand, identity and tone for your business that represents your offering.
- Solar Plexus Chakra: fully embodied wellbeing: looking after yourself so that you are grounded and embodied as a business owner, ensuring your needs are met and that you are taking care of YOU.
- Heart Chakra: sharing from the heart: producing marketing materials such as blogs, opt-ins, guest posts, videos, etc.
- Throat Chakra: conscious communications: PR and working with the media to get your aligned message out authentically and to a wider audience.
- Third Eye Chakra: vision and planning: having a vision and plan for your business.
- Crown Chakra: connecting to the field: aligning all your actions with divine guidance.

However, as I began to ground it and share these different areas, echoing my own entrepreneurial journey, it came to be equally, if not more, important to address the underlying things that can come up in business that relate to each chakra. The blocks, the limiting beliefs, the stories that hold us back from being fully ourselves and showing up to our full potential. The things that I had encountered on my business journey (and saw with clients), which were huge in terms of the inner journey I had been on and continued to come across on different levels as I continued to work on my business.

These blocks that can occur in the chakras are better known when it comes to wellness and there is a lot of wonderful information available if you want to dive deeper into them and understand them further. But, in this book, I share my perspective of how they come up in relation to business.

Working with the chakras is nuanced and multi-layered. So, although I give suggestions and tips for how to work with a block that might come up, please note it can sometimes be more complex than this, and you might need to look at other chakras where the block is, or try a few different things to support you.

The earth star and soul star chakras

In addition to the seven main chakras in the body that I include, I have also added in the earth star and soul star chakras, with the colours inspired by my training in the Colour Mirrors system.

The earth star chakra is believed to be about 12 inches below the feet and is seen as an anchor point for all the chakras in the body. Whilst the base chakra is a point for grounding the being, the earth star takes it further as it grounds all of the chakras into the earth, providing stability and wellbeing. I see the earth star chakra as a copper ball of light holding and grounding my being in the loving, rooted energy of the earth.

The soul star chakra is above the crown chakra and is known as the seat of the soul. It takes your spiritual connection deeper than the crown chakra and can be the point through which you connect to higher consciousness and your divinity. I see the soul star chakra as magenta, connecting you to the Divine and reminding you of the unlimited love that you are and have access to.

The earth star and the soul star are the anchor points for love and nourishment in your business, which are essential in my opinion. Without them you will not feel as supported, held, and connected as you can.

The earth star provides the Mother Earth energy and more grounded feel. Whereas the soul star provides the Divine Love, connection and support you can receive from Higher Consciousness. The body, with its seven main chakras, is in between the two, like a bridge between heaven and earth.

I hope that these two chakras serve as anchor points to you in your business and remind you that you are always held, loved, and supported from above and below.

Chakra messages

While I was writing this book, I kept getting guided to have conversations with my chakras. This was something totally new to me, but being one to totally trust the messages I get from my Higher Self, I went with it. I often talk to my heart and receive messages from it, I also sometimes receive guidance from my solar plexus area, so why would the other energy centres be any different? Throughout the book, you will find #ChakraMessages that I received. They contain inspiration, guidance, wise words, and reflections, which I hope are inspiring and helpful for you too.

I would also love to invite you to connect in with your chakras and really feel into their energy. I share a short visualisation for each chakra at the beginning of each section which might support you to connect with each of them. If you feel called, please also share the messages you receive on Instagram with the hashtag #ChakraMessages. Please tag me @empathpreneurs so I can feel your magic and share them too.

Chakra prompts

Below are some prompts you can use when connecting into your chakras to ask questions to support you in your business. Perhaps feel into the chakras that want to share something with you, as these will vary depending on what you are doing.

For example, if you are working on marketing and PR for your business you may want to tune into your heart and throat chakras.

- What messages do I need to know right now?
- What do you want me to create in my business at this time?
- How can I show up more in this area of my business?
- What do I need to support me in this area?

As an aside, if you don't feel anything when you connect to your chakras, please don't judge yourself. I didn't feel anything for a long time and it was only through different practices, letting go, and practicing over time, that I was able to. If this is the case for you, you could perhaps set an intention to connect with your chakras and trust that – given time – it will happen.

Past lives

I refer to past lives throughout this book as, for me personally, they have played a large part in my journey to accepting who I am and in releasing fears and blocks that have held me back in my business. You may not resonate with this or even believe it, all I ask is for you to keep an open mind and perhaps substitute the words with ancestral memories as a whole, which I also talk about.

To share a little bit of background, I have been interested in past lives for as long as I can remember. I have a vivid childhood memory of watching a movie at a friend's house and the woman in the movie was the reincarnation of someone. I remember journaling about it in my little diary I kept and being so moved and knowing that I had past lives too. It didn't come up again for years, but I would get flashes of experiences that felt like mine and like there was more to life than just me in this lifetime. When I opened up fully to the metaphysical world and began my deep dive into everything and anything I could find, (from Angels and numerology, to manifesting and energy healing) one of the first things I explored was past lives and reincarnation stories of young children who 'remembered' experiences. I also did numerous regressions inspired by the work of Dr Brian Weiss. I recorded all of my experiences and had some deep emotional releases.

When I began learning about colour in the magical system of Colour Mirrors this became even more cemented. I learned that colours can relate to specific past lives and that certain experiences might be showing up in our lives due to us being a mirror for it. A way to heal this and shift it entirely is to get back to the source which, as I discovered for me, was often past lives or the lives of ancestors.

I had some of the most profound breakthroughs and releases here, which totally shifted my inner and outer worlds in a matter of moments, and reaffirmed to me the power of connecting to this.

Being adopted, as a child I often felt disconnected from my family: I didn't look like any of them or have any of their inherited genetic traits. Through past life regressions I have connected with some of my adopted family in different lifetimes and had experiences with them, which reminded me how perfect it all really is. I was chosen because I am meant to be in the family I am in, and we have a lot more shared history than meets the eye.

If you are curious about past lives and feel that there might be more in here for you to explore, I invite you to try out the regression visualisation in the resources section, or get in touch with me.

Being a sensitive person in business

For a long time I hated being sensitive. I'd feel things so deeply: watching the news would make me so upset that I could be frustrated and holding back tears within a few minutes of having the TV on. The weather affects my mood in an instant: so if it was grey for days on end even in the summertime, I would feel it. Foods and drinks affect me more than other people: I can get super bloated, or sleepy, or hyper, or irritable, depending on what I consume.

When it came to working in an office I really struggled with commuting. I could feel drained in an instant or suddenly angry and not even know why. Until I learned tools and strategies to support me.

I dreaded networking events and would use alcohol and food to cope and get through the small talk, which I struggled with. I also used to take it so personally and feel it if someone was in a bad mood or annoyed. I was told on several occasions to grow a thicker skin.

I felt there was something wrong with me, and it was as though I was 'weaker' than others, when in fact I know I am super strong inside.

I've learned that being sensitive is actually a strength as it means I have to honour my body and being – if I don't, it will let me know. I can empathise, relate, and give so much compassion to others, which is invaluable as a coach, and in my opinion, as a fellow human. I can feel and tune into what clients need and support them on deeper levels. I am creative and able to connect to states of flow and magic that make me tingle.

I can feel this world so deeply that part of my mission is to help others and the environment. To honour this mission I have made big changes in my life – including going vegan, buying ethically and only what I need – and I will be contributing and encouraging others to do what they can for the environment and one another, for the rest of my time here.

Something else I now know is that looking after myself as a highly sensitive person requires a consistent commitment. It needs more spaciousness, nourishment, gentleness, and boundaries. It means changing how I look after myself on a weekly and monthly basis in accordance with the seasons and my own inner cycle. It includes playing with tools and techniques to help me with my energy levels, especially in today's fast-paced modern world.

I encourage you to consider how your sensitivity is a strength: every time you think you are too sensitive, or it is used against you, turn it around and declare why it is in fact a strength.

I invite you to use the hashtag #MySensitivityIsAStrength on Instagram and tag me @empathpreneurs when you use it.

As a sensitive being you offer your unique blend of empathy, intuition, healing, space holding, and beauty, which is so desperately needed at this time.

If you would like to download an e-book from a community project 'My sensitivity is a strength' sharing the experiences, thoughts and perspectives from a number of sensitive entrepreneurs you can find details for it in the resources section at the end.

Honour your sensitivity

Honour your sensitivity, see it as a strength. Let it guide and support you. Learn to work with it and embrace it as an integral part of your being.

#ChakraMessages

Earth Star Chakra (Vasundhara)

Earth star chakra (Vasundhara)

In this section you will find some suggestions for grounding and nourishing yourself and your business in a loving way. You might like to pick one suggestion at random to support you or work through one a day, week, or month, depending on what you need most right now.

Connecting to Mother Earth's love and support

The Earth is here to support you with your mission.
She is here to lean on, to guide you and hold you.
Her grounding and love are a balm for you whenever you need it, and even when you don't.

Hear her messages.
Feel her support.
Surrender to her wisdom.

As you ground your business and your mission, take the time to connect with her.
She holds a space of unconditional love and support that is here for you to receive at all times.

It's sometimes hard for empaths to feel like they belong on earth.
It's hard to feel at home here.
Allow her copper earth energy to soothe you and support you.
To remind you why you came here.
To hold you as you once remembered.
To be that mother we all need.

You may have felt or still feel separation, struggle and fear being on earth, but surrender it to this great mother and let her soothe your worries and anxieties. Let her feminine holding embrace you, tending to you with her strong yet gentle loving energy.

She is the love of all the Universe, the wisdom of all the ages.
She is a mirror of what you hold inside.

When you connect to her you will remember.

There is a visualisation in the resources section to support you with connecting to Mother Earth, to receive her messages and feel her support.

My vision

I want to live in a world where we are in balance with our rhythms and cycles, and those of this planet. Where we take time out to rest when we need, understanding that it's detrimental to our wellbeing to be 'on' all the time. Where we deal with the root cause of issues and don't try to numb or ignore them in an effort to move on and be more productive. Where less is more, and bigger does not mean better.

I want space to be held for all feelings and emotions, honouring everything that rises – the messy, the painful, the not knowing – as it all has something to teach us. There is space for all of it, not just the happy, positive side.

I want us to honour sensitivity and see it as a strength. It has the power to heal and create magic, if only we take the time to slow down and connect with it.

I want us to feel so in tune with our bodies that we know exactly what messages they are giving to us. That we are able to look after them and treat them as someone we love. So we don't disconnect from them and force them to do things we are told are good for us, but don't actually feel good. I want us to remember that we have everything we need inside.

I want us to embrace that we are a holistic mind, body, spirit being and need to nurture and nourish all parts of ourselves so we can thrive.

Building strong business foundations

Let your roots go deep into the ground.
Let them be infused with all that you are.
Let them be rich in experience and wisdom.
Let it take the time that it needs to.
The work you are here to do needs to be stable and grounded.

#ChakraMessages

Self-care for empathpreneurs

When I first began my wellness business it was fresh in my mind what it was like to work in an office. I had been looking after myself through small self-care actions to help me have a more balanced life in some of the areas I struggled with when it came to my health and wellness at work. Some of these actions were meditations and visualisations to listen to whilst commuting on public transport, healthy snacks and lemon water to keep me energised and hydrated, and I would make sure to take regular fresh air mini-breaks and breathe deeply throughout the day.

But when I began working for myself, I found that I almost totally stopped these self-care and wellness practices that had been so ingrained in my life. I was in a whole new environment working from home. I didn't feel the stress of having to sit at a computer screen with fluorescent lighting around me all day; I wasn't commuting, which was one of the things that drained me the most; I could easily make meals in my own kitchen; and I could exercise when I wanted.

I assumed that I would be fine as I had this new set up, which suited me on so many levels. I thought it would be easier to look after myself and include more wellbeing activities into my day. But I was wrong.

Ultimately, I found it all too easy to let work consume me and I didn't put any boundaries or time and space in place for me to prioritise my wellbeing.

- I frequently picked up my laptop first thing, still in bed, to get started on ways and places to market myself, then get stuck in that for the rest of the day, realising I hadn't done anything else by around 2pm. Then I would be starving and make some food. And then I would get stuck back into work, not realising the time, and it would be easy for me to make excuses not to exercise, knowing I prefer morning exercise.
- I put work first, thinking that it had to be a priority as it was just me doing it for me. If I didn't wake up early (which often

happened as I was sleeping late from too much screen time late in the night) I wouldn't meditate or journal, but instead feel guilty and start working straight away.

- I didn't cook fresh meals (like vegetable curries and stews) in batches the way I used to, as I thought I would have time to make myself food from scratch every day. But rather than doing that I ended up making more fast meals like pasta and sandwiches, which I didn't eat much of before.
- I also found it easy to have alcohol as a way to reward myself from working so hard. Something I had done throughout my working life. This led to a downward spiral for me in many areas.

Needless to say, those first few months were a bit hit and miss in terms of my self-care and it took me some time and letting go of what I thought my 'working for myself life' should look like before I was able to reconnect with my self-care.

My body was also not feeling good, I was putting on weight from less activity in general and the increase in bread and pasta, I was feeling more tired and wired from so much laptop use, and also stir crazy from living and working in the same room. I had to start making some changes. I had to start prioritising wellness. I had to walk my talk as a health coach. And, this time, in a way that suited my new life.

I knew *what* to do – that was never the issue. I needed to find a new routine and way of living holistically that worked for me.

I began to get to know myself as a person working for herself at home. I began to unravel what worked for me and how. I began to choose what I wanted my day to look like, not what I thought it should look like. I began to prioritise the things that made me feel energised so I could do what I wanted in less time. I put my wellness on an equal level with my work.

Doing this made me more focused and more aligned in my work. I felt more self-confident. I felt more committed to myself and my work.

Now there are times when work takes over if I have a deadline. But, as much as possible, I try to do things with time around them, so that I can make sure to prioritise wellness – it is essential to the work I do, and the work I do with empathpreneurs.

I truly believe we have to see our wellness and self-care as equal to our work in this world.

Here are some prompts that might support you to find a way to prioritise your wellness as an empathpreneur:

- When do you feel most energised in your day?

- When do you like to move your body? What time of day works best for you?

- What foods and drinks make you feel energised? Which foods and drinks deplete you?

- If you could do one thing to make you feel energised every day, what would it be?

- If you could do one thing to help you feel more rested each day, what would it be?

- What disrupts your sleep

- How much decompression time do you need at the end of the day before sleeping?

- What's stopping you, if anything, from committing to your wellbeing regularly? What can you do to support yourself here?

- What can you commit to daily, weekly and monthly when it comes to your wellbeing as an empathpreneur?

Clearing spaces in your business

Physically clearing your spaces is vital to feel nourished in your business.

Clearing your spaces also supports you with releasing the old and making space for the new. You feel good energetically and create more vibrational alignment in your entire being, as we are affected by the energy of all the things we have in our lives.

Here are a few areas where you might like to begin to literally clear the spaces in your business.

Physical letting go

What is it time to let go of in your business on a physical level? Some areas to de-clutter:

- Old client files
- Old training books and manuals
- Books that you no longer need
- Old financial records
- Old journals and notebooks
- Cleaning up your physical filing system
- Getting rid of old computers, software and/or hardware

Digital spaces

Another hugely important area is your digital spaces. As sensitive people we don't often realise how much of an impact this can have on us. Some areas to consider clearing:

- Streamlining your work social media feeds
- Perhaps leaving certain social media feeds
- Unsubscribing from newsletters
- Deleting old emails
- Deleting old photos
- Clearing your desktop

- Deleting apps on your phone/other devices
- Clearing client files
- Cleaning up your digital filing system as a whole

Working with the seasons and cycles in your business

In the western working world, it still seems to be the norm to work all hours, be available at the drop of a hat, and to prioritise work over everything else. Now, I know things are changing and there are of course exceptions, but, in my opinion, we are still tied to this very masculine way of working, which has dominated for so long.

When I worked full-time and had to be 'on' at all times if it was a working day and I wasn't on leave, I really struggled with this. I thought something was wrong with me as I found my energy levels lowering towards the end of the day (I am definitely a morning person), not wanting to talk to anyone around the time of my menstrual cycle, and feeling it much harder to motivate myself in the wintertime. I wondered why I couldn't be productive at all times, like it seemed everyone else was. I realised later it wasn't just me: many of us were simply giving the impression of being 'on' all the time as that was the expectation.

I would go through contrasting phases of numbing myself in multiple ways in an effort to ignore what I was truly feeling, or I would eat chocolate to stimulate myself and give me more energy to get things done if I was feeling tired. Then there would be times when I would eat well and exercise and would feel better overall and be able to keep up slightly more, but I still found myself unable to be 'on' all the time.

When I began working fully from home, I tried to do it that way to begin with. If I wasn't doing something, I would feel guilty and would make myself find something to do. I continued to see every day of the year, and every day of the month as the same: a time to be productive and doing something. But, being more in control of my own time, I began to see that even though I thought I felt I should work in this way, I was actually not achieving more. I was making myself feel tired and scattered and it didn't feel right to be doing this as a wellness coach – in terms of my message or regarding walking my talk.

So I began to unpick the way I was living and working even more. This led me on a journey, which subsequently linked into my wellness business, of the seasons and cycles, and how it is completely unnatural to be switched on and at your best all of the time. What felt so intuitive to me was in fact proven biologically and was fundamental to ancient healing systems such as Ayurveda.

Coming from the equator the seasonal shifts in a year had already been such a shock to me and I knew how much I was affected by the winter. So, as I had begun to look after myself slightly differently in each season of the year, I was inspired to approach how I worked differently in each season of the year too. It wasn't that easy to begin with, for example, there is still a 'go-go-go' approach in January, even though it is the middle of winter in the northern hemisphere, but I started to make small changes that honoured my needs, and which, in turn, supported my business.

Some of these changes were working shorter hours in the winter and more in the morning when it was light. I stopped feeling so guilty if I needed a nap at 3 o'clock in the afternoon and let myself do what my body was asking for rather than caffeinating and pushing through. I allowed myself to take more time off for rest and nourishment in the winter months and didn't do as much networking as my energy felt less outward. Over time I stopped launching things in the dead of winter and waited until the energy was rising. This led me to see my business year more in tune with a late winter/early spring start than a January one (at least while I was in the northern hemisphere), so I began to follow that rhythm.

I also began tracking my menstrual cycle, which totally tied into the seasons of the year on a micro-level. (As an aside, if you don't menstruate, this won't apply to you physically – but as an empathpreneur you might work with women who this applies to, so I think it's great to be aware of. It also fosters an inclusive vibe and overall more gentle approach to working). This is something I had always been acutely aware of: I have written down the monthly start date of every period since my first one all those years ago, so there must have been a deep knowing inside me that was aware of the power of it. But this time I began to track daily throughout my cycle how I felt emotionally, physically, energetically, creatively, and intuitively. I also began to take note of things that might affect my cycle such as how much sleep I was getting and what I was eating and drinking.

This awareness of myself has changed over time, as I have grown and evolved, but what I learned overall is that I am able to be super productive towards the middle of my cycle when I ovulate. I am quite happy being visible in my business at this time too. I also need less sleep and feel on top of my game. So if I schedule in a few too many calls I won't feel too bad at this part.

However, as I near my menstruation I need to start being more inward. I can't have too many calls in the diary, or I begin to feel overwhelmed, wired and tired. I am more intuitive and able to connect to my vision more clearly in this phase, so it's great for reflective journaling and getting ideas down. I am also creative in this part of my cycle so need to block out space for this, which is also one of my biggest forms of nourishment.

Learning these things about myself and how I can use them in my business has been such a magical experience and one that the old paradigm way of working simply doesn't allow for. It took time, which we often don't have in the working world, and an understanding that it is constantly evolving. When I first started tracking my cycle, I would still book in calls on the days when I wanted to curl up in bed. I would pop a painkiller and push through. Now I simply don't. I block out that time at the beginning of each cycle (as I am able to roughly see when it will be on a monthly basis) and honour the strengths of each part of my cycle as much as possible. It has been so liberating for me to take control in this fluid way, and such an affirmation and acceptance of myself as a woman in business who, yes, is cyclical and has needs that vary.

If you don't menstruate you can always use the moon cycle and chart what comes up for you in each phase of the moon. There are of course other cycles and seasons in our lives which we can use and let lead us in our businesses and lives, and I know many empathpreneurs do. Some of these are the planetary cycles – I know, for example, some people who will not do certain things during mercury retrograde. You might look at your circadian rhythm and what times of the day you work best, particularly if you are a man, as you are more attuned to this 24-hour cycle.

Working with the cycles and seasons in your business is about recognising and learning what cycles and seasons affect you and how you can use them to support you holistically.

If you would like to download a free cycle tracker to support you in your business, please take a look at the resources section at the end of this book.

Balancing the masculine with the feminine (In a way that works for you)

I personally have found that I have oscillated from the feminine to the masculine and back again, throughout my business journey. I have either been pushing and acting with little rest, or have felt overwhelmed and exhausted so had to stop for a while. There have also been times where I have been quite passive in my feminine and sat back without taking any action on ideas or towards my vision.

Our lives are always changing. You may find that at certain times in your life you have been more in your feminine and at others more in your masculine. The world certainly favours masculine characteristics in the typical working world, at least in my experience, and if this is the case you may start to become out of balance as you give more of this energy to what you are doing.

We need both the masculine and feminine energies in life. We can't have just one or we become unbalanced. For example: when we are creating something new in our lives, we may need the feminine energy to come up with or receive the ideas, allowing space and fluidity. But then the masculine energy is needed to take action and bring the ideas into physical form.

It can take time and energy to bring the masculine and feminine back into balance and, of course, awareness of these in the first place.

Here is a simple outline of some of the characteristics of the feminine and the masculine.

Feminine

The feminine is receptive, passive, more intuitive, inward.

The feminine in balance has these characteristics: flowing, nurturing, tender, kind, intuitive, creative, feeling, still, radiant, surrendering, sensitive, emotional, easeful, and allowing.

The out of balance feminine can be needy, co-dependent, overly-emotional, victim mentality, powerless, weak, manipulative, withholding.

Masculine

The masculine is projective, more expansive, outward.

The masculine in balance has these characteristics: confident, responsible, focused, strong, logical, stable, supportive, direct, clear, protective, boundaried, courageous, disciplined, capable, certain, and assertive.

The out of balance masculine can be confrontational, critical, abusive, unsupportive, unstable, dominant, aggressive, controlling, competitive, a perpetrator, abuse power.

- How do these characteristics of the two energies resonate with you? Do you feel like you may be out of balance in your business at all?

Here are some suggestions to help bring you into each of these energies.

Ways to embody more feminine energy

The feminine energy is connected to the sacral chakra – which is the creativity centre of your being. A few things you could do are:

- Wear more orange or have more orange items around you.
- Allow yourself to tap into your creativity in whatever way that means to you.
- Tap into your pleasure – what do you enjoy? What brings you pleasure?
- Be open to receiving. Ask for help or support from others and allow yourself to receive it without judgement or obligation.
- Be more playful.
- Allow yourself to collaborate and co-create with others.
- Trust and listen to your own intuition. Spend time in meditation

to connect to your inner wisdom.

- Listen to your body and what it needs. The left side of your body and the right side of your brain are connected to the feminine. So pay attention to anything that part is trying to tell you.

Ways to embody more masculine energy

The masculine energy is connected to the solar plexus chakra – which is the power centre of your being. A few things you could do are:

- Take action on things that you want to do or are being called to do.
- Put systems and/or structures in place to support you, so you feel held and safe in your endeavours.
- Tap into your inner warrior – do strength training exercises and stand in 'power' poses.
- Stand up and speak up for what you believe in.
- Have strong, clear boundaries in all areas of your life.
- Listen to your body and what it needs. The right side of your body and the left side of your brain are connected to the masculine. So pay attention to anything that part is trying to tell you.

The importance of community

Whilst being alone, with time and space to work on and in your business is A-M-A-Z-I-N-G, there is also much to gain from being in a community: a community with others on the same path, who get it. Get what it's like to be an empath entrepreneur. Get what it's like to feel on this journey:

- The days when you want to hide under the duvet.
- The days when you have to say 'no' to social events you used to say 'yes' to because you literally can't afford the transport fare.
- The times when you'd rather invest in your business than go out.
- The times when you'd rather go out than work on your business.
- Times when you wonder why you chose this path and think going back to a job would be so much easier.
- Then you remember that a job made you feel suffocated, so you re-energise and focus on your business.
- That feeling that you want to make a difference.
- That wonderful feeling when just one person lets you know that something you did or said affected them positively.

Having a community is such a support for all the things that come up in business, as well as for growth, accountability, learning, inspiration and much more.

Do you have a supportive community? I invite you to join the Empathpreneur community if not. You can find the details in the resources section.

Base Chakra (Muladhara)

Base chakra (Muladhara)

When it comes to the base chakra, this is the area of consciousness of the physical body. It is traditionally seen as the colour red and is located at the base of your spine. It grounds, anchors, and supports you as you engage with everyday life. It brings you into the present so that you are able to be in your life right here, right now.

Some of the blocks that can come up in the base chakra that might affect how you show up in business are:

- Issues around money and survival
- Not having clear boundaries
- Difficulty grounding your business
- Judgements about yourself
- Feelings of victimhood or martyrdom
- Not being present in your body

In this section, there are some stories, tips, and tools to inspire and support you. You might like to pick one at random or work through one a day, week, or month, depending on what you need most right now. Do whatever works for you.

But first, I invite you to connect with your base chakra by closing your eyes, or lowering your gaze if that feels more comfortable to you. Imagine a ball of red light at the base of your spine. Imagine it swirling. Imagine it getting brighter and bigger with each breath that you take in.

Are you able to connect with it and visualise it?

What do you feel?

What comes up when you connect to it? If nothing does, that's fine too.

Feel yourself here on earth, be present in your body.

#BaseChakraMessages

Embodiment

Embodiment and being fully present in the body at this time is an area I am hugely passionate about and definitely a part of my purpose here on earth. It has been my greatest challenge but also given me the most magic and meaning. It is what my first book 'Embodied – A self-care guide for sensitive souls' is about – my journey into my body. It is also one of the biggest blocks I have seen that comes up for empathpreneurs.

Lack of embodiment comes down to not feeling safe in a body. I have come across countless variations of this, from feelings of not fully incarnating or integrating with the body; leading isolated existences so as not to engage with what's really going on inside and not owning who you are; to escapism and wanting to avoid being in the body because of all the trauma and pain experienced.

The thing is: the magic is in being in the body.

Embodiment is connecting with the full range of feelings and emotions that we are able to experience because we are in the physical – learning and growing from it all. It's getting to know and trust the signs your body gives you as it is the intuitive part of your being. It's diving into the shadow parts and un-earthing the jewels that are your greatest strengths, as they can only be found in the darkness. It's the learning that our bodies are a microcosm of this planet and that we truly can find heaven on earth when we land fully in them.

Allowing yourself to be in your body and experience it completely is life-changing, literally. When you do this, you are able to address what comes up and be guided by your own body in how to release it. Your body tells you when something isn't aligned or isn't good for you and will affect you, so you can say 'no' to it. How you are feeling in your body is also the mirror vibrationally to what you will attract in your life.

When we are present in our bodies, we are able to shift our entire lives and create and manifest all we desire, and more. We need to be able to feel things in order to transmute them. So it goes without saying that not being in your body can have implications on your business.

I really recommend getting to know and connect with your body and its messages. Allow yourself to be present in your being. Feel your feelings and emotions. Give your body what it wants.

- How connected do you feel to your body right now?
- What could you do to support yourself to be more embodied?

As mentioned, if you do want to dive into this deeper, I share my story and what I did to escape my body, plus 52 self-care actions to support you with embodiment in my first book – 'Embodied'. You can find details for it in the resources section at the end.

Grounding the spiritual with the physical

Following on from being present in the body, I want to take it further and share some of my perspectives on why so many empaths find it so hard to ground the spiritual side with the physical, and what can support you to do this.

I find that it can go either way... Perhaps you have been immersed in the western working world with its emphasis on logic and systems, and find it hard to accept or even know where to begin with your spiritual side. You know it's there; you just don't know how to bring it into your life/business.

Or perhaps – and this is the one I find most common amongst empathpreneurs – you are fully connected with your spiritual side and you often prefer being in that space, but you find it much harder to be in the physical and bring your visions and gifts down to earth.

As an aside, you might find differences in these for different areas of your life (for example, I was more in the physical when it came to business and more in the spiritual when it came to my wellbeing).

Whichever category you fall into, they are both ultimately about separation and not bringing the spiritual into the physical. They are about not accepting that you can have both and be both: that you are a spiritual being having a physical experience.

When you have felt and experienced so much in life, it is often easy to feel unsafe being here on earth. It is easy to feel like you won't fit, what you offer won't be accepted, and that you will be judged. So it's easier to stay in the higher realms and not fully ground what it is you are here to do.

If you have experienced a lot of rejection in life, which is my story, with the ultimate rejection being at birth and disconnecting from source, it may feel like you will never be accepted in your physical form. Issues might come up around survival and being in your body. There may be a part of you that doesn't want to fully 'land' on earth, so as not to experience that disconnection and rejection any further. Ironically though, as you do this to protect yourself, you actually tend to attract more of it, which can show up in business as not clearly sharing what you do, not reaching the people you are here to serve, or not getting clients.

To shift this, you need to be fully present on earth. You need to accept and honour both your physical and spiritual sides. You need to accept yourself fully.

I invite you to begin to observe where in your life you feel that separation. You could spend some time journaling or reflecting on these prompts:

- Where do you escape or bypass your feelings? This could take the form of addictive behaviours or patterns.

- Where do you feel that you are not completely held and supported?

- Where do you not fully accept yourself?

- Is there a part (or parts) of yourself that you have shut down in any way?

- What could you do to begin to accept and honour both sides of yourself – the spiritual and the physical?

What are your beliefs around money?

When I began my entrepreneurial journey, I didn't appreciate how little I knew about money, or how much time, energy and money I would spend getting to know, un-pick and un-ravel this area for myself.

I have never been afraid of money – I like finances and spreadsheets, and I am organised so I find it easy to keep on top of expenses, outgoings and incomings. It never even occurred to me that this would be an area I would need to learn more about. You really don't know what you don't know! But what was new for me was the whole world of the energetics of money. The soul of money. What money represents. All the beliefs about money I had taken on throughout my life and that had cemented in my being. The layers and nuances of meaning I had put in place. I had no idea money could be related to how I felt about myself, my worth, or my value.

Both the practical and energetic sides are equally important and if you have blocks when it comes to the practicalities of your money, I strongly recommend you do what it takes to get on top of it. Keep track of everything and do it regularly if that's what you need. Get help if that's what it takes.

I am going to talk more on the inner energetics that can come up around money and how I have experienced them. Money blocks can come up in a few of the chakras as it is such a huuuuuge area; they can come up and affect many areas that you might not even realise.

There are many, many people who teach about money blocks and many areas you can dive deeper into. What I share here is only a fraction of what you can go into. But I hope it lays the foundation for further exploration, if it calls you.

Before I begin, what do you think about money? How do you feel about money in your life and business right now? How comfortable are you talking about money?

Take a moment to see what comes up for you.

Money can bring up so much in our modern society.

We fear it.
We love it.
We steal it.
We beg for it.
We want more of it.
We avoid it.
We lie about it.
We borrow it.
We save it.
We create beliefs with and around it.
We think that it is limited.
We think it is the root of all evil.
We associate it with greed, control, and power over others.
We think it makes us separate from others.
We feel guilt around it.
We feel shame around it.
We need it for survival.
We want to get rid of it.
We hoard it.
We donate it.
We will do anything for it.

Do any of these resonate with you?

There are so many different beliefs, viewpoints, and stories that we have created as a society when it comes to money. These beliefs and stories can then create a lot of internal blocks, as you begin to associate money with some of these things. These then may prevent you from receiving or welcoming in money, for charging your worth, or even allowing yourself to ask for it.

We have been born into a system that is steeped in beliefs, and we have been led to believe that there is only a certain amount of money available: money is finite. We believe we have to fight or struggle to get our bit of it, and we have to compete with one another, due to this limitation.

We have also created beliefs about ourselves based on experiences involving money throughout our lives. For example, as a child you may have been given pocket money, but then had it taken away if you were naughty. Thus, creating the belief that when you are bad you won't receive money. This might then translate into you not thinking you deserve money later in life if you feel bad about yourself.

We have given meaning to money based on things that we grew up hearing, or situations which we may have been a part of, or witnessed, or been told about. An example of this from one of my clients was a belief that you couldn't make money doing what you love. She had been told by her parents that she had to have a 'proper' career in order to make money and there was no point to her trying to follow a more creative path. She had loved fashion all of her life and had taken courses in it, but never felt she could do anything with it because of that block and fear that she would be penniless if she followed her heart.

But this is simply not the truth. Money isn't any of these beliefs we have created. It is an energy and a tool that we use, and we don't need any of this extra baggage we have given to it. In fact, these kinds of beliefs create a vibrational mismatch in us and can be one of the biggest factors which can limit you in your business.

We can change how we feel about money. How we see it and what it actually is. We can change our beliefs and create new ones. New empowering ones which work for us all.

Here are some journaling prompts to begin to unpick your beliefs about money.
(I recommend coming back to these prompts regularly, as once you begin to un-layer beliefs, more come up).

- What are some of the things you grew up hearing about money or in relation to people who had money? Some examples could be 'money doesn't grow on trees', 'you have to have money to make money', 'nice people never get the corner office', 'money is the root of all evil', 'it isn't spiritual to make money'.

- Looking at each of them individually, ask yourself: is it true? How do you feel about this now?

- Now looking at your life today, what are some of the experiences or memories you have with money that may have caused you to create a belief? What is the belief?

- How do you feel about these situations now? Can you see how you have created a story around what happened?

- How can you begin to create a new empowering belief here?

- Some suggestions are:

    - Find examples from your or someone else's life that show you the belief isn't real.

    - EFT or tapping can help to release old beliefs and embed new ones. There are many wonderful EFT practitioners who can guide you with this.

    - You can also do some inner child or ancestral work to go back and re-write the belief. If you would like to explore this further, you can reach out to me through my details in the resources section at the end.

- To take it further and continue to reveal beliefs you may have created about money, really begin to notice how you think about money today and what your thoughts are around it.

- From observing how you think about money today, what beliefs have you created? How can you begin to turn them around?

Forming a new relationship with money

Now that you have started to look at some of your beliefs and begun to change them, I want to encourage you to begin to form a new relationship with money. This will be ongoing, particularly as new systems come into our society and changes are being made globally when it comes to how we exchange and buy things.

Simply explained, money is just energy and a part of our current system that has been created to place value on a good or service for exchange. That value will vary depending on need in society, and the individual and their own needs and preferences. To give a simple example, if you love reading you will place much higher value on a book and be willing to pay for it, than someone who doesn't. Or look at how the value of hand sanitiser went up during the Covid-19 pandemic.

What we don't take into account are the many things that contribute to society that we don't place a monetary value on for exchange – things such as kindness, how we care for others in our family, holding space for a friend, even a smile to a stranger can have an enormous effect on their day, which ripples out.

This, in my opinion, has contributed to many people, particularly empathpreneurs, not owning their worth and value when it comes to what they offer. I go into this in more depth later in the book.

Money isn't the big thing we have made it out to be. It is simply there for us to use as a value for exchange. And I want to encourage you to feel deeper into what that is, and how you can begin to see it differently.

I invite you to tune into the energy of money. Feel into the energy behind what it physically is. Feel into its essence.

- What comes to you? What do you feel? What do you see? What does it have to say to you?

- How could you begin to see money differently in your life?

Connecting to the energy of money

When I connected to the energy of money, this is what came up for me:

I am flow.
I am connection.
I am magic.
I am joy.
I am love.
I am here to enhance your life.
I am here to support you.
I am here to create with you.
I am here to be your partner.
When we show love and respect for one another, all things are possible.
Let's have fun together.
Let's make magic.
Let's create wildly and big.
Let's know no limits.
Let's love, let's flow, let's play.
Let's do this together.
Let's believe the impossible and make it real.

This feels quite different from the heavy, limiting beliefs I had previously experienced and felt around money. This feels expansive, full of possibility, and an exciting place to create from.

Feelings of victimhood or martyrdom

Do you ever feel like you have to play the martyr or victim in your business?

Do you find that you over-give and always put yourself last?

Do you give away too much for free?

Do you feel guilt and shame if you aren't struggling in some way in your business?

Do you believe that you are here to serve others at your expense?

If any of these things come up for you, I have found it may be linked to past-life, ancestral or childhood memories. In particular experiences which were steeped in dogmatism or founded on a strict religion.

The key here is getting to the root cause of when the belief started – in this or another lifetime – and to heal it or re-write it.

You can listen to the regression meditation in the resources section to see if it can help guide you to the root cause – beforehand set an intention to be guided to where the belief began – and then perhaps spend some time journaling on these prompts:

- What happened to cause you to believe that you must adopt a victim/martyr role in your business? Do you have any ideas about this? Trust what comes up for you.
- How does being in this position make you feel?
- Is this reason still appropriate to your position now? Is it supporting you in any way?
- How can you begin to change it?
- What can you tell yourself now? How can you support yourself to re-write it?

Holding on to judgements

This is a huge area and can sneak into your actions and behaviours without you even noticing as it is such an ingrained part of our daily lives. Many of us have been forming judgements, which then lead to beliefs, for our own (or ultimately our ego's) protection and survival for years. Think back to when you were a child and someone did something to you that was painful or not nice in some way. You would have formed a judgement about them, perhaps about others similar to them, and situations like that, so you could look out for it in the future, protect yourself, and to try and prevent it from happening again.

Here's an example from a client who was just beginning her entrepreneurial journey as a virtual assistant. She had a couple of bosses who she just didn't click with. It was as though everything and anything she did for them wasn't up to their standards, she didn't get enough done, she didn't know enough, she wasn't organised enough, she wasn't fast enough.

Both of these experiences happened close to one another and occurred while she was working for charities. Even though what she experienced with these two bosses was in complete contrast to her experiences with some of the other people she had worked with (also within charities), who valued and appreciated her and her work, she formed a judgement about working with and for charities.

Needless to say, she developed a bit of fear around working for charities and wouldn't approach them for months, even though that's where her heart was. She also judged herself on some of their comments and took them on board about her standard of work. It took her a while to build up her confidence again.

Holding on to judgements does not serve you on the empathpreneurial journey (or in life, for that matter). They can stop you from continuing to show up. They can hold you back from expressing yourself. They can prevent you from reaching the people you are here to work with.

You need to be able to alchemise these judgements, so they become a part of your growth on the journey.

Yes, we are all going to have experiences in our lives where we feel like we are failing, feel like we aren't good enough, or feel like we are wrong, but it's up to us to see that these experiences are actually leading us in the direction we are meant to be in.

This was reaffirmed on my Colour Mirrors training: there is nothing to judge in life as every experience we have ever had has been FOR us. It has all helped us be who we are today. It has all served us in some way, even if it didn't feel good. So, if it is all perfect, why would we judge any of it?

- Where are you holding on to judgements of yourself or others, and how can you see the lesson and gift in them, so they do not hold you back?

Owning your shadow parts

I think this one comes up more for empathpreneurs as we feel so much and our businesses can play such an integral part in our lives. Consequently, it is important to honour and acknowledge all of you for your business to be successful.

Some of the blocks that can come up in business are absolutely shadow parts too, and I have gone into some of these in more depth throughout the book. Now I want to talk about triggers that can come up in business and how they are often a clue to a shadow part of you. I will also share with you a really powerful method I use to help me (and clients) get to the bottom of shadow parts and transform them.

Some of the things that might trigger you in business are:

- Comparing yourself to others on social media
- Other people's pricing
- How other people show up – for example on their website, in videos, in their marketing
- People demanding too much of your time
- People not wanting to pay for anything

Some of this can be about the ego, not feeling like you are doing enough, wanting to be further ahead, and comparing your stage in business to someone else who may have been in business a lot longer. As well as these, there can often be underlying shadow parts too, which ultimately are all a reflection of something going on inside of you at a deeper level.

When triggers come up for me, I take the time to go into them and to see what part of me they are bringing to my attention, so that I can bring the light onto it to support and look after myself.

An example I will use to illustrate this, which has come up again and again, is being triggered by what others are sharing and a feeling that what I am sharing is not good enough. Each time it comes up I ask myself if it is about my ego, and it can be in part or in full. If it isn't fully, I begin to dive into it, asking myself these questions: 'What am I feeling beneath the trigger?' This can often be things like not-enough, lack, frustration, jealousy, competition, is it all worth it, loneliness, emptiness, disconnection, fear of abandonment or rejection.

Then I ask myself 'What is the emotion I am feeling beneath that?' Things that can often come up here are fear, despair, sadness, and anger.

I then dive deeper into these emotions, feeling each of them individually in my body: sitting with them; acknowledging them; noticing the colour, size and shape; really being with them and holding the space for them. I then start to ask them more questions. Some of the things I ask are:

- What is going on for you right now?
- When is the first time you felt like this? What was going on then?
- What do you need right now?
- What will support you?
- Are there any practical steps you can take?
- Is there anything blocking you from releasing?

I trust and allow what comes up, sometimes journaling on the responses, and then give myself what I need.

It is often easier to be held through these times, so please do reach out if you need support. You can check out my resources page at the end or get in touch with someone you trust.

Once the shadow parts are brought to the light they can be alchemised into your greatest gifts and shift your entire vibration, but you have to be brave enough to go into them.

Some of the gifts I have received from going into my shadow parts have been strength, courage, more flow and connection to my intuition, being unattached to what others think of me, deeper self-love and self-acceptance.

Having boundaries in business

Having boundaries in business is an area that many empaths struggle with. It can come up in different ways but one of the most common is over-giving. Often empaths give a lot of themselves, and want to help everyone and be available to support others as needed. Especially in the early days of a business, when you are just getting started and are keen to jump on any opportunities that come your way. If this isn't managed with a little bit of awareness it can easily lead to over-giving and spreading yourself too thin, which will affect your health in the long run. You will likely end up feeling overwhelmed and burnt out.

In this section we will look at some of the more practical boundaries in your business. We will go into some more of the energetics behind boundaries in the heart chakra section.

Work/life balance

- Do you have set hours that you work?
- When do you switch off?
- How do you ensure this happens?

Emails, social media and other forms of communication

- How and when do you communicate with your clients? Be clear with your boundaries and what times you will be available to answer to clients. Then stick to those boundaries.
- How do you decide what opportunities you say 'yes' to and which ones you say 'no' to? You may want to create an Avatar for 'someone' in your support team, before you even have a team. This can actually be you to begin with so that you have someone you can 'use' to answer on your behalf if difficult decisions have to be made. For example, it can be easier to pretend to be someone else saying 'no' to a request to do something if it doesn't align with you. Over time it may get easier, or you can hire a freelance assistant or a team member to do this for you.
- The email inbox can be a nightmare for many empathpreneurs

and can take up a lot of your time and energy. How can you manage your inbox so that you don't get overwhelmed and 'waste' time checking emails and responding at all hours? You could only check emails at certain times, for example. Or set up rules to file certain emails so that you can come to them in your own time. In time you can always get someone to do this for you.

- When do you go on social media and how do you manage comments, messages, etc? I plan this in accordance with my cycle. I know that I get particularly triggered by social media and am more likely to compare myself to others at certain times of the month, so I don't scroll, or I stay off of social media as much as possible during these times. What will work for you? There are also platforms that can support you practically with this e.g. you can schedule your social media in advance so you don't have to log on all the time.

Other people's opinions

- How do you create boundaries for yourself on social media and when receiving feedback from others? If you get attached to everything that is said about you, you may find yourself on a rollercoaster of approval seeking. How can you look after yourself so that this doesn't happen? One way is to keep track of only the positive and constructive feedback you get. You could keep a file of testimonials to remind yourself of your amazing work.

Boundaries for your self-care

- What practices help you to feel your best so that you can serve from a place of being filled up in your business? When will you schedule them into your business?
- Do you need to allow extra time before or after certain things in your business? For example, after client calls you may need 30 minutes to decompress, or before prospective clients you may need an hour to feel into the energy and ground yourself.
- What do you need most to ground your energy regularly and to do the work you are here to do? Is it a whole day blocked

off each week to be offline – in nature – where you can come up with new ideas? Or you may want to have the mornings to yourself for self-care, family, etc, and to start work later in the day?

- What support do you need to establish better boundaries for your self-care? This could be support anywhere in your life or business.

A good thing to do is to keep a note of the times you feel overwhelmed. Then ask yourself what has contributed to this feeling and what can you do to support yourself and change this.

Sacral Chakra (Svadhisthana)

Sacral chakra (Svadhisthana)

The sacral chakra is located a few centimetres below your belly button and is traditionally associated with the colour orange. It is your creativity centre, connected with your feelings and emotions. It is connected to your relationships with others and how you relate to intimacy. It is also the area in our bodies where we tend to hold on to trauma.

Some of the blocks that can come up in the sacral chakra that might affect how you show up in business are:

- Inability to receive
- Blocks in your creative flow
- Holding on to past traumas
- Disconnecting from your life force
- Feeling easily overwhelmed

In this section, there are some stories, tips, and tools to inspire and support you. You might like to pick one at random or work through one a day, week, or month, depending on what you need most right now. Do whatever works for you.

Before that, I invite you to connect with your sacral chakra by closing your eyes or lowering your gaze if that feels more comfortable to you. Imagine a ball of orange light in your sacral area below your belly button. Imagine it swirling. Imagine it getting brighter and bigger with each breath that you take in.

Are you able to connect with it and visualise it?

What do you feel?

What comes up when you connect to it? If nothing does, that's fine too.

Flow to the rhythm of life, feel yourself in tune with this vibration.

#SacralChakraMessages

What stories are you telling yourself that might affect your capacity to receive?

I grew up in Kenya where I was given a lot. I had an abundant life, with a beautiful house and garden, summer holidays to visit family and friends in the US, Canada, and Europe. There were many wonderful things I took for granted and believed were always going to be there.

But as I grew up, things changed. I went to do an art degree at a university in London and quickly realised that my upbringing wasn't the norm for many people, most people in fact. I was around a lot of cliché 'broke art students' and I felt guilty about who I was. I began to feel different and separate from some of the new friends I had made.

Meanwhile, when I went back to Kenya for holidays and to see my family, I began to see my life there in a dramatically different light. The contrast between wealth and poverty seemed to be exacerbated. I had always been aware of it but had also been in a 'protective bubble' growing up. The contrast hit me so hard, I even decided to do my final first year (foundation) art project on it and spent time looking into children in slums and comparing them with myself. Needless to say, I felt it all. I felt the unfairness and the inequality. It felt too much and I began to hate that I had so much in comparison to those who had so little.

Something deep down in me changed at this time. I began to resent having more than others and, looking back, I realise I began to reject who I was and what I had been given. I started to pay for everything for friends when we went out. I thought that it was my obligation to help them as I had more. This became a pattern and I would give, give, give, always being the one to say, "I'll pay", and feeling guilty if someone wanted to give me something.

When university finished I had to start making my way fully on my own. I was on minimum wage to begin but, after I'd graduated, I was also given access to a trust that had been left to me by my mum, who had passed away when I was eight years old. This meant that, once again, I was in a different financial position to my colleagues – who I was spending more and more time with. I continued to offer to pay for everything when we went out together, even paying for taxis for them to get home if it was late!

I also began telling myself that I would rather have had a mother than the money, and I remember feeling completely disconnected from it. As you can imagine, I went through my trust fund pretty quickly. Even when it ran out and I was in the exact same position as others – earning just my salary – my beliefs and behaviours had become ingrained and I still felt an 'obligation' and 'responsibility' for everyone else. As I began to earn more, I was still able to pay for others, but I also managed to get a loan, credit cards, and have an overdraft during this time.

It was only when I began to hit the beginning of my rock bottom and I left my work (loan spent, credit cards maxed, and living at the limit of my overdraft), and with only minimal income from one part-time freelance job, that I HAD to start changing. I had six months where I couldn't find more work, so I couldn't pay for others. I could barely pay for myself, and there were weeks when I could barely afford food, let alone rent.

This was one of the hardest times in my life but, on some level, inside, I also felt that it was what I deserved. It was my turn not to have anything. I also felt some sort of nobility at being how I perceived others to be. I wanted to make it on my own, from the bottom up, and not from using what had been handed to me.

Over the next few years, this is what showed up for me. It was like my tap of abundance that I'd had growing up was now shut off. No matter how hard I tried with business – and I knew what to do and tried a lot – it wasn't making me money. It was only when I began to unpick these many stories and layers, releasing and letting them go, that things started to shift and change.

I slowly learned to love who I am. I stopped judging myself and accepted what I had been given, seeing it as a gift rather than a curse. I began to feel worthy again: worthy of living an abundant life and not just one where I am scraping by. I began to attract people who wanted to work with me and pay me. I learned that my being in lack and scarcity doesn't help anyone, least of all me.

- What stories might you still be telling yourself that affect YOUR capacity to receive?

Blocks to receiving

Do you have any blocks to receiving that might be stopping you from bringing in financial abundance for your offerings?

This area can be linked to different beliefs and programming that might not even come from you in this lifetime. Blocks may be from a past life or ancestrally in your lineage and, if that resonates with you, you can find a short regression visualisation in the resources section to help you begin to uncover them.

As I shared in the previous story – 'What stories are you telling yourself that might affect your capacity to receive?' – I had lots of issues around receiving and felt that I didn't deserve to have anything, or that by having I was taking away from others. There wasn't enough for everyone. I had created a whole story around this from the upbringing I had as a more privileged person growing up in a country with extreme poverty.

When I began my business, I gave everything away for free, and continued to do so if someone showed any hesitation around paying for anything. It got to a point where people stopped buying from me. I even had friends say to me that they questioned why anyone would buy from me, as I just gave it away anyway.

In addition to this:

I have connected to past lives where I have been killed for having money.

I had a very Catholic upbringing and felt a lot of guilt and shame around money.

When I was a child my primary caretaker stole from our family and was fired, which was devastating for me. Later in life I realised that, if I didn't have any money, nobody could steal from me and I might not attract people who I cared about and then might lose.

As you can see with many of these things it can be layered and there can be a few reasons, so here are a few prompts to help you begin exploring how open you are to receiving.

- Who are you NOT to receive?
- Who are you serving by not charging what you are worth?
- How do you push money away?
- What else do you push away?
- How does it feel to charge what you are charging for your offerings?
- What would you say to someone you deeply admire who was offering and charging what you are?
- What do you notice here?
- How would it feel if you doubled your prices?
- What do you notice here?
- What do you feel might happen if you do become rich and receive more financial abundance? How will your life change?
- What do you feel you need to enable you to open up to receive more?
- What support can you get here?
- How does it feel to ask for help?
- When you receive help, how does it make you feel? Can you receive openly, or do you feel guilty or like you are expected to do something in return?

Doing it all alone

I see so many people struggling and pushing on alone.

Trying to do everything, or be everything to everyone. Dealing with so many things at the same time – attempting to multi-task.

Feeling anxious or low and not sure how to feel better, so masking these feelings with painkillers or substances. Feeling low in energy, or constantly stressed and unsure how to change it, or just accepting it as a part of life.

Being so overwhelmed, and trapped in the rat-race, that your weeks begin to feel like a hamster wheel with no way off.

I did this for MANY years. I thought I should be able to do it all alone, that there must be something wrong with me for not being able to figure 'it' out on my own. That I was weak or incapable if I asked for support. Or that I'd be seen as more capable if I did it alone.

I can tell you now, that it is total BS!

Receiving help is life-changing. We're meant to do this journey with support. You will get through things so much faster and feel so much better, quicker. I have received help from coaches, healers, therapists, friends, family, courses, mentors, teachers... you name it! For things like help losing weight, to working on my business, to healing trauma, changing my career, and more. And I have no intention of stopping – I now want to feel supported at all times.

There are so many solutions and ways to get help within your budget if you just start looking.

Please don't soldier on in silence, get the help YOU need for whatever you may need it for. Something small perhaps to start, that might give you some more time for you... Start where you are at, with what you need.

- What support do you need?

- What action will you take to get it?

Holding on to past traumas that may affect how you show up in your business

This area can be huge and unique to each of us. What might come up? What might be needed to support you to release it? What might be the root cause?

It can also relate to different chakras, for example, you may experience heartbreak or a traumatic experience that involves your intuitive gifts, but I include it in the sacral chakra as this is the area where we tend to hold on to trauma.

Trauma held in the sacral chakra can show up in your life as an inability to fully accept and receive the feminine part of yourself (and we all have both feminine and masculine sides within us). This translates into business as being unable to be wholly you and unable to show up in your beauty, sensuality, creativity, and flow. So you might hold yourself back from being creative, you might not allow yourself to be seen, you might not allow yourself to embrace your intuitive gifts.

This certainly came up for me in multiple ways and in layers, as is normally the case. But ultimately I felt unable to receive myself fully for who I am. I felt disconnected from my femininity and self as a woman, which added to my visibility issues (which I share more about in the throat chakra section), and was reflected in how I received (clients and financially) in my business.

One of the reasons I knew I had issues in this area was that I was unable to connect visually to my sacral chakra. In general, I have a strong connection with my other chakras – I feel their energy, I can bring coloured light into them, I can make the light bigger and stronger, I can feel where there might be blockages. I have, however, always struggled to do this with my sacral chakra so I knew intuitively something was going on there that was blocking me.

I have also always felt that I have held on to ancestral trauma and past life experiences, as I have just known that certain reactions I have felt or beliefs I have had about myself were not mine from this lifetime. They didn't make sense and I have done a LOT of work unravelling layers and going back into experiences to get to the root cause, but nothing came up that resonated or helped me.

Eventually, I got to the bottom of it: during a past life regression, I connected visually and somatically to what had previously happened through one of the most powerful experiences I have ever felt in my body, releasing it in the process and re-writing the story to a new, beautiful, empowering one which I am now left with.

The experience I needed to heal was of a past life in India where I was abused by several men and was left feeling like I wasn't enough, that I couldn't show my beauty, I couldn't speak up and I couldn't be fully me – nor was it safe to be. The release happened through a good few hours of constantly crying followed by body convulsions and noises that I didn't know I was capable of as I felt the experience and allowed my body to release it. I then re-wrote the ending to one where I was admired, respected, loved, and even slightly worshipped by the men. I felt the beauty, love, and joy of that new situation and how safe it was to be in my entirety and show off who I am. This changed something on a deep level and I am now able to do this in my life and business like never before. I felt connected to my sensuality and myself as a woman for the first time. I feel able to show up as me fully. I feel the ripples of this shift changing all areas of my life.

- Does this resonate with you?
- Do you feel there might be past traumas that you are holding on to that are holding you back?
- How can you support yourself to release them?

I really recommend getting support to hold you through this process if you are newer to this work.

Your pain can be alchemised

Your pain can be alchemised into your greatest gifts.

#ChakraMessages

Blocks in your creative flow in business

How do you feel about creativity and business? Is creativity something that you are able to connect to and use in your business? I know quite a few entrepreneurs who, particularly at the beginning of the entrepreneurial journey, didn't believe that creativity is a part of having your own business.

I invite you to feel into this and whether you believe creativity and business can go together? What beliefs do you have around this?

Creativity is integral to the entrepreneurial path. It is the part of you that: comes up with new ideas; finds ways of sharing that work for you; tunes into the flow and magic of the Universe; and is linked to expression.

Blocks in creativity can come up in a number of ways, two of which are feeling creatively uninspired or fearing ridicule or shame for expressing yourself creatively.

As with many blocks, you might find a number of reasons why these come up for you. I will share some examples from my own experiences and generally from working with others.

What you are trying to do creatively may not be for you. It could be that what you are trying to do is not aligned with your purpose, so you are intuitively not connecting with it.

But something I have found that comes up again and again is a belief that you are not creative in any way, and as such fear expressing yourself creatively, due to being told something negative about your creativity earlier in life.

This often happens in childhood and may have been something like 'failing' an art project or getting a low grade in a more creative subject. Or perhaps you grew up with parents who didn't put much appreciation onto the arts and more creative subjects, so you were never praised in these areas and stopped trying or thinking you were any good.

I have my own version of this from my art degree, which I failed the first time. From then on, I didn't believe I was creative in any way. I didn't think I could be creative ever again, so I placed all my attention into furthering my business skills and my more analytical and logical side. I wouldn't dare to paint or even write for myself for years, and when I did write at work, I did it with so much trepidation.

Any form of creating was difficult for me for a long time. I looked to others to see how they used their creativity in their businesses as a way to inspire and guide me, whilst I completely dampened down any hints of my own creativity.

I eventually found my creative flow through other forms of creating, namely taking photos for my Instagram feed and doing lots of cooking. As I began to connect to the flow that comes from creating, I remembered that we are all creative beings. I was a creative being.

This helped me to unlock my creative flow and connect to my creative power in all the ways it wanted to come out. I began to write again: for myself, for my business, for others. I began to follow my own creative vision in my business. I even began to paint again using my art in some of my graphics.

- How can you support yourself to connect to your creative flow? You could think back to what creative activities you loved doing as a child, and use that to inspire you today.

- What beliefs or stories have you told yourself that are stopping you from connecting to your creative power?

Solar Plexus Chakra (Manipura)

Solar plexus chakra (Manipura)

The solar plexus chakra is the power centre of our being and is located in the middle of the body a few centimetres above the belly button. It is usually associated with the colour yellow. It is connected to your worth and power as an individual and when it is balanced you feel strong, empowered and a sense of self-worth. It is also known as the stress area of the body and you may find yourself turning to addictions when it is out of balance.

Some of the blocks that can come up in the solar plexus chakra that might affect how you show up in business are:

- Feeling out of control in your life
- Feeling fear and stress easily
- Being led by the ego more
- Feeling insecure and unconfident
- Not owning your worth or true power, playing small
- Holding on to things that are no longer serving you

In this section, there are some stories, tips, and tools to inspire and support you. You might like to pick one at random or work through one a day, week, or month, depending on what you need most right now. Do whatever works for you.

Firstly, I invite you to connect with your solar plexus chakra by closing your eyes or lowering your gaze if that feels more comfortable to you. Imagine a ball of yellow light in your solar plexus area at the middle of your body. Imagine it swirling. Imagine it getting brighter and bigger with each breath that you take in.

Are you able to connect with and visualise it?

What do you feel?

What comes up when you connect to it? If nothing does, that's fine too.

Own your worth.
Shine your light.
You are here for a reason.
Allow yourself to be YOU.

#SolarPlexusChakraMessages

Owning your worth

In the masculine way of living that currently dominates our working world, I feel that worth has been given to what we 'do' and more qualitative things, far more than to what and who we are or more intangible things. This, in my experience, has presented a block in many empathpreneurs who tend to work in more healing, creative, intuitive and less tangible (on the outside) professions.

The masculine, more left-brain services such as finances, western medicine, law and business are the ones in which people tend to claim their worth. They know what they offer, as in many cases it can be physically measured, and can charge accordingly. It seems to be easier to claim the value here as these services have been established for longer (at least in our more recent history).

As always, there are exceptions and I know many people in more intuitive, healing professions claiming and making their worth financially, but there are many empathpreneurs who don't know the value of what it is they offer, and so don't charge their worth and end up feeling burnt out and depleted. For me, this has come up consistently and, as always, is multi-layered.

Absolutely, if you are in the early days of your entrepreneurial journey, you may have lower prices, give things away at a discount, offer free sessions, or do exchanges with others perhaps in return for testimonials. For some empathpreneurs, depending on what your values are, you may continue to offer discounts to some people, or perhaps do pro-bono work to support those that aren't so well-off, and I do this and support it. But there also comes a time when we need to realise the value in many of the services that are offered by empathpreneurs and begin to own it and claim it.

Think of all the things you might offer just by being you. If you are a coach or a healer who holds space for others, you will likely offer many of these qualities and gifts without even realising it. Things like being a good listener, making others feel safe and heard, allowing them to open up, providing empathy and compassion, sharing your intuitive wisdom, sharing and giving authentically from your heart and experiences. It's only when you take a step back, or ask for feedback from people you work with, that you realise how powerful and life-changing some of these things are and that they aren't physical, tangible things that can be easily described.

One way to start owning your worth is to see it all as energy. After all everything is energy – even money. Think of all of the energy you put into something – perhaps your products, or the ways in which you prepare and show up for the people you work with. When you do this, your mind can begin to see the true worth of what you do.

There might also be ancestral or past life wounds around owning your worth. For women in particular, there is a lot ancestrally (and currently – let's be honest) around being inferior, or 'only' being housewives or caretakers. The qualities that are used in these roles are not given as much worth by society as a whole, which has a ripple effect on how you might view yourself and your value.

If you do feel there might be more here that is with you from a past life or in your heritage, I really recommend allowing yourself to feel into it, either alone or with someone to hold the space for you in this area, so that – as well as feeling it – you can begin to understand where it might be coming from and heal it through acceptance and love. We are who we are today. Yes, our past experiences – whether within us or through conditioning – make us who we are, but we also have the power to re-write our future by claiming our worth.

The world needs a fundamental shift in how we value qualities that are more feminine, and I believe that, as empathpreneurs, we are the ones to help initiate this change. Gone are the days of the broke healer, the starving artist, and the over-giving creative. These professions – each with their unique qualities – are truly magnificent and are so needed to bring the feminine back into balance with the masculine. And, for this to happen, the value of these gifts needs to be claimed and owned.

- Where might you not be valuing yourself?

- Where are you not charging your worth for what you do, or who you are?

- Write a list of all the qualities you give or use in your business – things that you can't necessarily see or measure. If you had to put a price on these in terms of all the energy you give out what would it be?

- How does this make you feel?

- What changes will you make based on this exercise?

An invitation to connect to yourself as a child

Often as children, before life happens and the world tells us who we are and how to behave, we know our worth and value. We came into this world unafraid to claim our brilliance, our gifts and talents. It's through experiences and conditioning that we start to dim our light and hold ourselves back.

- Does this resonate for you?
- Is there a time in your childhood when you were fearless and owned who you are?
- When you didn't question your value or worth?

I invite you to spend a moment connecting with that little version of you. The little you before the world told you who you were.

Think back to that person...

- What age were you?
- What were you like?
- How did you know your worth and value?
- How did you show up in the world?
- What did that little version of you want to be when they grew up? It might have changed now, but were there any doubts that you could be that?
- Ask that little you if they have any messages for you right now.

Holding on to things that are no longer serving you

One of the constants that comes up on this journey is needing to let go of things that are no longer serving you.

As you refine and try things it is essential to let go of what might not be for you, what might have been for a lesson only, in order to make space for the new ideas and creations to come in, and to open up to the path that is yours.

This can relate to holding on to situations, people, ways of working, patterns in your life that affect how you show up, systems and processes, or even stress and fears. There are so many things that you can refine and let go of in and around your business on a regular basis.

I have let go of a number of things over the years that weren't serving me for different reasons, but all ultimately affected me energetically. When that happens I cannot be the most me I am here to be.

Things I have let go of include: friendships; drinking alcohol; eating dairy and meat; judging myself (I still do this a bit, but it is a lot less than when I began my entrepreneurial journey); a number of group coaching programmes I created; social media handles and feeds; fears around speaking up; and work partnerships that no longer feel aligned.

Here are a few prompts for you to begin to check in and let go of what may not be serving you.

- Is there a pattern or behaviour that you are holding on to in your life that stops you from showing up fully and as you know you are here to do?

- Are you holding on to any old ways of working that aren't aligned?

- Are you trying to sell a programme or offering which just isn't gaining traction and truthfully doesn't feel good in your being?

- Are there are any people or situations in your life which make you feel stressed and which you can begin to let go of?

- What else are you holding on to that is affecting your business and you know it is time to let go of?

Self-sabotage through patterns and behaviours

Something I experienced a lot of in the early days of my business was self-sabotage. I would regularly fall into patterns and behaviours which stopped me from showing up and committing to myself and to my work fully, particularly if an opportunity to grow – but that pushed me out of my comfort zone – came up.

This is a shadow part, which I shared more on in the base chakra section, but I want to speak about it explicitly as it was so linked, for me personally, to not owning my true worth and power, and what I knew deep inside I was capable of.

My biggest self-sabotage behaviour was drinking alcohol. I had used this behaviour a lot throughout my previous working life and in general. I would binge drink when I was presented with opportunities to speak in public so that I couldn't and wouldn't be able to show up fully. I then had an excuse for myself and would sometimes even cancel the speaking opportunity. This happened a couple of times, then the opportunities stopped coming in until I was ready inside to show up fully for myself.

I would drink whenever I finished a rewarding client session that I was nervous about. Needless to say, all the positive feelings I felt from supporting the client would be replaced by a hangover and self-loathing. So it felt like I was starting from a deficit and having to pull myself back up again and again, to get back on track with my energy, how I was feeling, and how I could show up in my business.

I wouldn't allow myself to feel how good it could get. How good I could be. I would always make sure I brought myself down in some way when I started to feel any excitement, or possibility for expansion and growth, that meant me accepting my own worth and value.

This went on, to varying degrees, for a couple of years, but finally began shifting on a deeper level when I joined the women's circle I previously talked about, and had to show up. I knew I had to do it for myself. I had seen visions of myself speaking on stages, showing up, writing books. I knew I was the only one stopping myself.

Change didn't happen overnight; it was a gentle yet challenging, multi-layered approach involving many different things including support from others. Ultimately I began to believe in myself more as I showed up and committed to doing what I said I would do – for others and myself. I dealt with many of the layers I had built up which affected my confidence and self-esteem. I started to really push myself out of my comfort zone and do the things that scared me. This helped to show me that I could do what I knew I was capable of. I knew I couldn't do these things and drink, so this became something I only did when I had complete time off. Eventually, I stopped altogether to fully commit to myself and my business, and this is where I am today.

- Are you self-sabotaging in any way to prevent yourself from owning your true power?
- What patterns and behaviours are you still turning to, to avoid your true potential?
- What could you do to begin to change this?

Fear of your own power

I felt afraid of my power for a long time. Afraid of what I might be capable of, afraid of being controlling over others, and afraid of the damage I might do if I was in my full power.

Looking back, it seems crazy that I felt like this. I know that I would never (knowingly) want to hurt someone and the last thing I want to do is control others. But this is something I feared and that held me back for a long time. I know that many others can relate too.

Through diving deeper into the feelings I felt around power and fear of my own power, I was led to a few past lives where I had abused my power and controlled and manipulated others – in Atlantis, in Medieval times, and also in Egypt. I was still carrying so much guilt and shame around this and so that was what power meant and truly felt for me.

Through releasing and healing some of these memories, along with a deeper understanding that every lifetime happens as it is meant to – every experience has been for that person to grow and expand – I was able to begin to shed some of my fears so they no longer hold me back from my authentic power today.

If this resonates, perhaps you might be holding on to lifetimes where you abused your power or were at the receiving end of it.

Another side to this is a fear of your greatness. As Marianne Williamson famously shares, and to paraphrase: it is the fear of being in your light, it is fear of your brilliance and your talents. I feel this can happen for a number of reasons, one of which is the feeling of wanting to belong. As children we learn that if we don't do things a certain way, or perhaps over-excel, or exceed others, we may not be liked. If this happens we might get more attention than the other kids, or they might be compared to us, which affects their self-esteem and makes them feel less than, causing them to not like us. So we then feel ostracized or left out, feeling like we don't belong. There are many reasons why you might fear showing your greatness. If this resonates, what's yours?

Fearing your power and greatness could also be linked to the way you were brought up, or through your ancestry. You may have been told not to show off, not to speak up, or not to shine.

- How can you begin to re-write this?
- Who are you serving by not stepping into your greatness and authentic power?

You are here to serve a purpose as you

You are a Divine being who is here to serve a purpose with YOUR gifts, talents and authentic power.

#ChakraMessages

Connecting with your authentic power

Power in today's world (and our most recent history) often comes from the ego, from a place of manipulation, control, image, greed or competition, to name a few areas.

Authentic power is something quite different and comes from a knowing deep within, from trusting yourself fully, from not competing with others, from leading with care and compassion for others.

Here are a few prompts to help you show up from your authentic power.

- Do you compare yourself with others?
- Do you let others influence what you do and how you show up in your business?
- What do you fear will happen if you do it your way?
- Tune into your solar plexus or your heart, what does it want for you? What business does it want to have? What life does it want?
- How can you begin to take action and bring this into your life?

You are a powerful creator

You are a powerful creator and what you choose for your life and business is up to you.

#ChakraMessages

Feeling the fear in your belly

Often in business there will be things, especially in the early days, that you have to do but that aren't in your zone of genius, or that bring up fears in you, which you feel particularly in the belly or solar plexus area.

I have had clients who absolutely detest doing the administrative side of things, for example, keeping track of expenses. I had a client who had so much fear around being on social media for her business and resisted it so much. I had one who hated sending out newsletters and would spend days perfecting and tweaking them before finally hitting that 'send' button.

All of these things are helpful, if not essential, to an online business and there are ways to help yourself if you feel the fear about any area.

I recommend getting support with the area that brings up fear, or that your dislike, as soon as possible. Even if it is only a tiny amount to begin with, it will help you to move through that area and feel supported, which is an added bonus.

You could also re-frame the activity so that you connect to the reason why you are doing what you are doing (which links back to your purpose). For example, you could be doing the financial side of your business to connect you with your numbers and help you grow your business. You could see social media as a way to be creative and have meaningful conversations with aligned people and potential clients.

Find your way of doing things and do them that way. This could be working and scheduling tasks in accordance with the moon cycle. Or it could be taking yourself offline for a day and batching content for blogs.

Another thing you can do is reward yourself for small achievements and for doing the things which are harder for you. A dear empathpreneur friend of mine sets a 20-minute timer for doing the things she doesn't enjoy so much, does the activity in 20-minute blocks of time, and regularly celebrates how far she has got.

Do you trust yourself as a leader?

How does this question sit with you?

You might say that you want to lead and make a difference, but do you actually trust yourself as a leader? Lack of trust can often hold you back from being the leader you know you are here to be, without even realising it.

Some of the things that came up for me around this were not walking my talk and feeling like a fraud – still indulging in unhealthy habits and behaviours when I was trying to be a health coach. I know no one has to be perfect, but there was a definite misalignment here for me and, as an empath, I have to be in integrity in order for me to claim I can do something.

I also didn't want to lead in the way I had seen others lead: generally men and women who were more in their masculine power. I saw them as being much louder and strong personalities, able to lead from a more dominating position. This always felt off to me, and I know is not something I can do, so I didn't trust myself to lead in that way. I am much more aligned with leading from a place of gentle strength and inclusivity. Today there are many different types of leaders, and once you set the intention to find leaders you resonate with, the examples come flooding in.

One other thing that came up was thinking I didn't know enough, or that I had to know everything – whatever that might be. This was definitely an old paradigm way of leading and came from my ego. I was scared I'd be caught out not knowing something or not having an answer if anyone ever asked me anything. I was caught up in that for a while; until I learned you only need to be a couple of steps (even just one) ahead and that we are all learning and growing on this path.

I had to change many of the beliefs I had around what I thought a leader should be, as well as dive into where I was sabotaging myself from fully stepping into that energy.

- How can you learn to accept the leader YOU are?
- What kind of leader are you or do you want to be?
- How can you own who you are as a leader?

You weren't born to fit in

You weren't born to fit in.
You were born to make a difference.
To bring this world back into balance.
To stand for love, beauty, compassion and light.
To create the change so needed at this time.

Dare to be different.
Dare to do it your way.
Dare to lead from your authentic power.
Dare to lead from your truth.

#ChakraMessages

Heart Chakra (Anahata)

Heart chakra (Anahata)

The heart chakra is traditionally associated with the colour green, and is connected to love, relationships, and your connection with yourself and others.

Some of the blocks that can come up in the heart chakra that might affect how you show up in business are:

- Struggling to share your feelings
- Not feeling safe to share your truth and vulnerabilities
- Not having clear boundaries, and over-giving
- Not loving or feeling passionate in your business
- Feeling envious and jealous of others
- Being unconnected with yourself, with love and with life
- Not feeling safe to give and receive from your heart

In this section, there are some stories, tips, and tools to inspire and support you. You might like to pick one at random or work through one a day, week, or month, depending on what you need most right now. Do whatever works for you.

But firstly, I invite you to connect with your heart chakra by closing your eyes or lowering your gaze if that feels more comfortable to you. Imagine a ball of green light in your heart area in your chest. Imagine it swirling. Imagine it getting brighter and bigger with each breath that you take in.

Are you able to connect with and visualise it?

What do you feel?

What comes up when you connect to it? If nothing does, that's fine too.

Let the love in.
Know how loved and lovable you are.
Let love lead.

#HeartChakraMessages

Sharing vulnerably

Sharing vulnerably can be so scary but also so powerful. I think we are all looking for stories that are real, deep, and genuine. Stories that connect us to another, make us feel like we aren't alone, and that someone else gets it.

As an empath, I know how much feelings and emotions connect me to my world. When I am moved by something or have an emotive connection to it, I feel much more invested. It's hard for me to fully get something until I feel it in my being.

Sharing in business, I learned, is the same for me.

When I began sharing in my business in the early days as a health and wellness coach, I would share pieces on top tips for sleep, how to prioritise your daily habits, self-care tips for wellness at work and so on. Whilst these are all really valuable pieces of information and useful to people who need them, they didn't connect me to my audience.

I intuitively knew there was more I could be doing here and, in my morning journaling and meditation, I kept getting the message to share more vulnerably. To share my stories and my own experiences. I was getting ideas for the specific stories I could share. The ones that had a message or that had changed me in some way, and I had begun to write some of them down, but they were sitting unshared in journals and on my laptop.

This totally ties into feeling safe to be seen, and I had a lot of fear coming up around this. But eventually, I surrendered to my intuition. I also read Brené Brown's book on vulnerability and knew this was what I had to do. As I was moving more towards self-care at the time, I decided on a piece about my drinking habits. In it I shared incredibly vulnerably how I had behaved, how I felt, and how – with self-care – I had moved through it to get to where I was now. I put the piece into my newsletter template for that week, but then waited days, feeling all the feels before actually sending it.

I felt like I would be judged for sharing about my drinking: perhaps people would think I was an alcoholic; maybe they would think I was being self-indulgent by talking about this when there's so much other big stuff going on in the world. I questioned if my sharing would actually be helpful for anyone else. What if I was too much? Or not enough? What would friends who knew me and that I had been with at that time think of me? I went through every thought imaginable that could and almost did stop me from sending that newsletter.

I did send it though. Once I pressed the button I remember feeling sick to my stomach and more exposed than ever before in my life.

But what happened next surprised me. I got replies from people, for the first time ever in my year of sending out blogs, saying how much they related. Thanking me for my honesty. Grateful to me for sharing my story. Telling me that it had really moved them. I was quite blown away and felt such an opening in my heart. It was an affirmation for me that I was on the right path.

From then on, I began to share more of the stories I had been writing down just for me. More were bubbling up to the surface and I just kept on sharing. Each time the feeling of being naked and exposed decreased a little bit and it eventually felt like an act of service and something I just had to do.

Something that helped me was detaching from any outcome. Sure, it was flattering for my ego to receive kind words, and heart-warming to know I was supporting others, but I knew it was also helping me to shed my layers: to release the stories that had been holding me back, and to let them go from my being.

The journey that sharing vulnerably took me on wasn't what I expected. Through sharing my stories I found the confidence to finally write my book 'Embodied', which took my sharing vulnerably to a whole new level as I combined many of the stories I'd already written and added even more. Whilst being one of the most healing experiences of my life – one which supported me on multiple levels in terms of where I was holding myself back in my life and in my business – it also enabled me to reach more people: more soul clients and connections that have enriched my journey more than I thought possible, and continues to.

I've had people message me and say that they want to work with me as they relate to my story. I've had articles with my story in them published in multiple different media outlets and blogs online. And I have been asked to share my story at many speaking opportunities.

Daring to be vulnerable and to be seen for my truth and my story has connected me to who I am and what I am here to do on a whole new level. I truly believe the world needs more of it. For us to move through our experiences and reach the truth of who we are here to be, we have to face the depths of ourselves and shine a light on them.

- Where are you being called to share more vulnerably?

Share your truths

Share your truths, your vulnerabilities, your stories, your real-ness, for it is in this that you will connect to others and find your way.

#ChakraMessages

Surrendering to the journey of self-love

The journey of self-love is intertwined with the empathpreneurial one. As empaths, we feel so much that it is almost impossible to separate what happens in your business with how it relates to you. I know from being an empath myself, working with empaths and those who aren't empaths, the difference in how they react and respond to things that happen in their business.

For example, in a situation where perhaps a client decides to pull out or gives some negative feedback, those who aren't empaths are able to separate the facts from feelings much more easily and not get stuck in where they might have gone wrong. Empaths will feel more of the emotional nuances and may let it stop them or spend a lot of time questioning it, going into it and reflecting. Perhaps giving it more time and energy than it deserves.

Absolutely, as you continue on this journey, you get better at not taking things so personally and are able to move through situations which might not feel so good, you are able to see the lesson in it all and learn and grow from it.

But another suggestion is to surrender to the journey of self-love from the beginning. See it as equally important to your success in business, not least as a way to look after yourself as you deserve, but also from a vibrational standpoint.

The more self-love you are able to give yourself, the more you will be able to build resilience and look after yourself as you need to be looked after, to do the work you are here to do.

Self-love is a non-negotiable in my opinion and needs to be regularly topped up so that you know your worth and your value. You let it lead and don't waste time going into things that you know aren't here for you. It connects you to your truth, and showing up from that space is life-changing.

- How can you give yourself more self-love: daily, weekly and monthly? What do you need to support you?

Having meaningful connections

This is so important: as much as I love my alone time and can spend days creating and working without others, I know how valuable it is to connect on a heartfelt level with others who are on the same path.

It's having others who will champion you as your personal cheerleaders and give you the truth when you need it. Who will hold your heart and really listen when you are having down days, holding space for you to figure out what you need. People who will mirror back to you the love that you are and the truth that you hold inside of yourself.

This can absolutely come from working with a mentor or guide, who is aligned with you. But it can also be with supportive friends, which I have been blessed to have as well.

I honestly think that as empathpreneurs we need this, and I know from when I didn't have it, how much harder I found the ins and outs, and ups and downs of this journey.

- Do you have someone that you can share with openly who supports you on this path?

Not having clear boundaries and over-giving

I also talk about this in the base chakra, and it can, of course, come up in other chakras. But here we are looking at boundaries around the heart.

It's really common for empaths to over-give and not have clear boundaries. Does this resonate for you?

Where does it feel out of balance and like you are giving more than you are receiving? Take a moment to answer this.

I would like to invite you to tune into why you are doing this more deeply.

- What is the truth behind why you are allowing yourself to not have clear boundaries, why you may be over-giving?
- What are you seeking?
- What do you fear?
- What do you think will happen?
- What is the feeling beneath it all?
- What is the truth beneath it all?

Once you get honest on this you can begin to understand what is driving it, and how it makes you feel.

Often, we over-give to seek approval, validation, and love from others. This of course might not be the case, but if it is, I recommend digging deeper into it and asking yourself where it is that you don't accept and love yourself.

Not loving or feeling passionate working in your business

One of the fastest ways to stop yourself in business is to not love or feel passionate about what you are doing. Or to be doing something because you think it is the right thing, or that you should be doing it. This connects to your purpose and your reason 'why' you do what you do: it's hard to show up for something that doesn't have meaning for you.

One of my clients was an artist who started making products to sell because it made commercial sense. She was investing a lot of her time, energy and money into doing this, but her heart wasn't in it at all. She wanted to be an artist – spending time creating and making because that was her passion. Needless to say, it wasn't long before she felt burned out and overwhelmed by it all and had to make some changes to support herself and be more aligned to where her heart really was.

- How does this feel for you right now?
- Do you love or feel passionate about your business, or at least parts of it?
- If not, how can you change this?

Tied into this is having a work environment for yourself that you love or that you are at least comfortable in. How you feel about your workspace can make all the difference to how you show up. As an empath, you might be particularly sensitive to clutter, noise, colours and the view.

- How do you feel about your current working environment?
- What changes could you make to love it even more?

What does your heart need today?

Here is a short meditation to help you to take a moment for yourself to connect with your heart. You might like to place one or both hands on your heart space as you do this.

Feel the energy of it. Notice the colours. Notice the shape. Notice what you notice.

Breathe into it. Softly. Deeply. Compassionately.

Feel it beating. Feel it giving you life force. Feel it holding you.

Feel the stillness. Feel the connection. Feel the trust.

Ask your heart, what does it need today?

Trust the answer and do what you can to give it to yourself.

Do this meditation as often as you need. I recommend daily: first thing in the morning and whenever you need to connect back into your truth and authentic self.

Throat Chakra (Vishudda)

Throat chakra (Vishudda)

The throat chakra is traditionally associated with the colour blue and is connected to your communication and expression: speaking up and being heard. It is connected to how you voice and express what you need, what you are passionate about, and what you want.

Some of the blocks that can come up in the throat chakra that might affect how you show up in business are:

- An inability to speak up and share your voice
- Talking all the time and not listening
- Not being able to express yourself clearly
- Not believing you have anything valid to say
- Not voicing what you need in your business

In this section, there are some stories, tips, and tools to inspire and support you. You might like to pick one at random or work through one a day, week, or month, depending on what you need most right now. Do whatever works for you.

To begin, I invite you to connect with your throat chakra by closing your eyes or lowering your gaze if that feels more comfortable to you. Imagine a ball of blue light in your throat area. Imagine it swirling. Imagine it getting brighter and bigger with each breath that you take in.

Are you able to connect with it and visualise it?

What do you feel?

What comes up when you connect to it? If nothing does, that's fine too.

Speak up.
Express yourself.
Let yourself be heard.
What you have to say is so valuable.

#ThroatChakraMessages

Fear of being seen

For a long time, one of my biggest fears was being seen. I hated photos of me and wouldn't dream of being on camera. I wouldn't even talk to family on video calls. So when I learned that to market myself as a coach I would need to show my face, I resisted for a long time. It made sense to me logically as I was my business and people needed to get to know me in order to know if they wanted to work with me. But I couldn't bring myself to even share a photo of me for the first six months.

I felt I was being vain or that I would be judged in some way. It felt way too vulnerable to share myself out there and this was a definite block to me being visible in my marketing.

In contrast, when I was little I loved being the centre of attention, I wanted to be an actress and I didn't think twice at having to go on stage or be filmed. In fact, I sought it out. Many of my childhood home videos (from growing up in the 80s) are of me saying 'Daddy, daddy, please film me' and I'd be there talking straight to the camera, pretending I was a princess or giving my viewpoint on something. In school, I went for all the verse speaking competitions and won many. I would also love being the lead in the school plays.

I remember things started to change when one of the other children in school told me I couldn't always be the lead and should give someone else a turn. I also distinctly remember overhearing one of the teachers saying I was too tall and didn't look right for a main part on one occasion. So I began to think something was wrong with me. Something in me clicked that day and, after that, I started to go for the obscure parts – the witch, the evil one, even male roles or the narrator where I wouldn't have to be seen. Eventually, I stopped trying out altogether and shut down that dream.

This visibility fear grew stronger and I have vivid memories of being so petrified of speaking aloud in university, I'd miss that day, or make excuses at the last minute so I wouldn't have to do it. When I started work and was involved in a pitch or had to share an idea in a brainstorm, I would get so nervous my stomach would be a complete mess and I wouldn't be able to eat or drink anything beforehand.

I remember one time being signed up to do a presentation training course, I got drunk the night before and showed up so hungover I was throwing up throughout and blanked when it was my turn to present. It was like I was subconsciously sabotaging myself as well as proving to myself that I wasn't able to speak out loud in front of others.

What helped me begin to change this was joining an online weekly women's circle. I remember the first call I had with the woman running it at the time; I had to show up on Zoom on video. I was literally shaking and went through a tonne of excuses in my head beforehand about why I shouldn't or couldn't do it. Why I wasn't right for it. Why now wasn't the time. But something in me persisted and I did the call. Afterwards I felt a flood of adrenalin and a little tiny part inside of me remembered how much she loved to be on camera. So I joined a group call with all the women, there were 14 others and we all had to take it in turn to share.

This was a whole new level of nervous and, again, I went through in my head the maaaany reasons why I wasn't right, why I should postpone, make my excuses. But, again, that little part inside of me made me do it and I had my turn to share at the end. There was so much power in that call. Listening to other women speak their truth, share from their hearts, and also comment in the chat box that they related to what I shared when it was my turn, made me feel so seen and heard. I felt safe and accepted for being me.

I gratefully joined the group and for the next 16 months of my life showed up every week on camera and shared. After nine months I even lead my first call, leading the opening meditation, holding the space, and doing a reading at the end. It pushed me to my limit again, but inside I knew something felt so right; a part of me felt like I had done this before, that I was meant to be doing it. Although there were mistakes and it was a bit clunky and I read the meditation that I wrote, I did it. It opened the door for me to keep doing it, keep practising. A couple of months later I even held my first online self-care for the soul workshop with paying guests and have continued ever since. Each time it got easier.

I also began to share more of me in my marketing. I'd record short videos and share photos of me. This journey continued and still does, but every time I shared something it got easier and I felt able to do more.

One thing I realised is that I had all these big fears about being judged or ridiculed. Most of the time people are so concerned with what's going on for them that they don't even notice. Also, in the beginning, hardly anyone would see my posts, so there weren't many comments, and the ones I did get were from supportive friends, who continue to support me when I show up visibly online (and behind the scenes).

Sharing in a safe space with people who were on the same page and whom I didn't feel any judgement from was life-changing for me. It helped me to build up my confidence, feel like I was enough and that I wasn't alone. We all need others to be our cheerleaders and to accept us as we are, otherwise it can feel scary and intimidating putting yourself out there visibly.

- What do you need to support you to share more visibly?

Expressing yourself

I find that expressing yourself and allowing yourself to express are closely linked with feeling safe to be seen and can come up as a block in the throat chakra. Some of the ways this might show up in your life are not speaking up, not sharing your opinion, not expressing yourself creatively, not speaking your truth, or holding yourself back from sharing and expressing in any way.

When I first joined the women's circle and was petrified of being seen, I was actually even more afraid of expressing myself. I got used to being seen quite quickly and felt safe amongst others who didn't judge me, but it took me longer to actually begin to speak up and share my opinions, or my intuitive feelings and thoughts. I would often hold back and let others speak and share before me. Some of the reasons that came up for me were: I wasn't confident in what I had to say, I didn't want to be wrong, and I didn't want to be judged. A small part of this does come from me liking to feel into everything first and know where I stand, but I realised that even if I got an intuitive feeling about something quickly, I wouldn't say anything. I began to notice that others would share the same thing that I was thinking, and this showed me that what I had to say was valid.

As I started to reveal the layers of what might be holding me back from speaking up and expressing myself, some of the things that came up for me were childhood, ancestral and past life memories, and traumas. This was the case for a few of my clients who also had fears around expressing themselves fully, with a common theme being persecution for speaking up.

I have had clients who, during regressions, have connected to a memory of being burned alive, hanged, cut at the throat, strangled, drowned, or thrown off cliffs simply because they shared their voice in some way. One client in particular, who knew deep down that she is a writer, was having huge fear around sharing her words with anyone. She connected so powerfully to a memory of being burned alive that her entire body was also burning up as she regressed. As she learned why she was being burned for speaking out against the status quo, she realised she had been betrayed and sold out by her husband, and labelled an outcast by everyone she loved. As we worked together, holding her in love and acknowledging the experience, accepting it for that lifetime, and giving her what she needed, she felt a huge release in her being and started to share more vocally and visibly within days of our session.

On a separate note, a practical way to support yourself to speak up is to simply take action and let yourself speak up. Over time you will stop caring about what others think and stop judging yourself for not saying the 'perfect' thing. I have done this, and the more I did it, the more confident I felt. I realised that we are all more concerned with what we are each saying than what someone else is saying. I didn't need to be so worried that I was being scrutinised. The more I accepted myself, the less I judged myself also.

- What are you afraid of when it comes to expressing yourself?
- What might be holding you back and how can you begin to support yourself here?
- How can you begin to let yourself express more?

Now is the time to speak up

Let the voices of your ancestors be heard.
Let the wisdom of your soul be revealed.
Now is the time to speak up.

Let the words speak through you.
Let them alchemise the pain into messages of hope and creation.
Now is the time to speak up.

Let yourself be a channel for these messages.
Let yourself be carried by their truth.
Now is the time to speak up.

#ChakraMessages

Connecting to a past life around expression – prompts for you to begin to explore this

(Please get support if you need, as this can be intense, deep and emotional work).

I recommend finding a quiet space where you can relax and will be uninterrupted, so that you can allow whatever wants to come up.

To begin, think about what it feels like to express yourself in this lifetime. Perhaps imagine you are in a room about to share something with a group of people. Maybe think of a certain time when you had to express yourself in front of others. Allow yourself to go there, feeling it in your body. Then, when you have connected to that memory, I invite you to answer these prompts.

- What comes up for you around expressing yourself?
- What fears arise?
- What emotions arise?
- What feelings and sensations do you have in your body?
- What colours do you see?

Now, can you allow yourself to go back to the first time you might have felt these things? Gently lower or close your eyes and feel back to when that might have been. Trust intuitively what comes up. It could be in this lifetime, it could be in another. Just allow yourself to go backwards in time, and to land wherever the first instance of it appears to you.

- Where are you?
- What's happening?
- What do you feel?
- Ask yourself what you need. How can you give it to yourself in that situation?

Voicing what you need in your business

Are you able to voice what you want with other people in your business, be it team members, people you are collaborating with, external suppliers, or clients?

This might come up around boundaries, asking someone to do something a certain way, saying 'no' to something, saying when you aren't happy with something, asking for help... There are many times and opportunities in business to say what you need but this can be a hard area for empaths to embrace.

It's one I certainly relate to, and I have had clients with issues in this area too. One client was a wonderful healer and offered so much but had such difficulty putting up boundaries with clients – she would always say how she was going to tell them that she was unavailable on weekends, but she struggled to do it. Another one struggled with saying what she wanted with suppliers. She found it hard to say if something hadn't been done to her liking and in alignment with her vision.

- How do you feel about this area? Are there any places where you find it hard to voice your needs?

First of all, I encourage you to look at the reason or reasons beneath why you are finding it hard to voice what you need.

- What are you afraid of happening if you do say what you need? What comes up for you around this?

Here are also a few practical tips to support you.

Voicing what you need can get easier over time, as you get more confident through the experience of doing it. So start small and keep adding to it, strengthening this muscle.

- What is one area you can start to voice what you need? Begin here.

You could set criteria for yourself in a specific area so that you have clear boundaries around what you will and won't accept. Then if you need to speak up and declare your needs, you have a benchmark from which to go from and can feel more confident in this.

Look at the bigger picture of it all.

- What are you gaining from not voicing your needs?
- How is this holding you back or stopping you from having the business you desire?
- What have you got to lose by voicing your needs?

Third Eye Chakra (Ajna)

Third eye chakra (Ajna)

The third eye chakra, located between your eyebrows, is associated with the colour indigo or royal blue and is connected to your inner wisdom and knowing, your intuition, foresight, vision and decisions.

Some of the blocks that can come up in the third eye chakra that might affect how you show up in business are:

- Not trusting yourself and what you are here to share
- Not trusting your inner wisdom
- Fears around being psychic or intuitive
- Inability to focus and stick to your vision

In this section, there are some stories, tips, and tools to inspire and support you. You might like to pick one at random or work through one a day, week, or month, depending on what you need most right now. Do whatever works for you.

I invite you to connect with your third eye chakra by closing your eyes or lowering your gaze if that feels more comfortable to you. Imagine a ball of indigo/royal blue light in your third eye area between your eyebrows. Imagine it swirling. Imagine it getting brighter and bigger with each breath that you take in.

Are you able to connect with it and visualise it?

What do you feel?

What comes up when you connect to it? If nothing does, that's fine too.

Trust yourself.
Trust your path.
Trust that it is all unfolding perfectly for you.

#ThirdEyeChakraMessages

Holding the vision

Having a vision that is compelling and motivating for you is undoubtedly one of the best ways to keep up the momentum and move forward in your business.

This is definitely harder in the beginning of the entrepreneurial journey as you may not be as clear on where you want to be, you may want to experiment, and you may know what you don't want but are less clear on what you do want.

This is why having a reason – knowing your 'why' – is so important as it inspires you to keep doing what you are doing, to keep reaching out, to keep showing up, and to keep moving through the bits that bring up fear in you.

My vision has changed throughout my entrepreneurial journey, and that's okay. In the beginning it was about bringing wellness into the workplace and seeing offices have more rest, honouring the seasons and cycles, cutting out junk food, and giving employees more emotional and mental support. It was a strong vision and one I still fully believe in, but as I was no longer working in an office and really didn't like going into one, there was a definite mismatch there. I tried and tried to hold on to it, I even tried to change it to supporting sensitive people in the workplace to align it more with myself but, eventually, I had to accept that it's not a vision that I am necessarily here to actively play a part in.

Where my heart lies is in changing the system at a grassroots level, eventually leading to a global scale, and empathpreneurs are the ones that will do that. So, my vision has changed to reflect that now. It is one that makes me more motivated than I have ever felt. I have dived deeper into areas that have held me back before and moved through them. I have followed my intuitive guidance on action to take, with no procrastination – unlike before. I am passionate about this work and honoured I get to do it.

- How do you feel about your vision? Are you able to hold it? If not, perhaps it needs some tweaking. Does it reflect where you are at now?

This is the message I received at the beginning of the Covid-19 lockdown. It helped me reconnect with my vision and might be supportive for you as I feel that this time was the start of the great awakening, which empaths are here to play a part in:

Now is a wonderful time to re-connect with your vision for what you would like this planet to be like. Yes, there is a lot of fear, overwhelm and uncertainty. But change is most often brought about during these times, and you have an opportunity now to create the world you want. Spread your messages of beauty, love, healing and compassion. Support others and show the world that there is another way, rooted in kindness, sustainability and love.

- What is the kind of world you would like to live in?
- What values do you stand for?
- What changes would you like to see made?
- Why?
- How can the work you do contribute to bringing into existence what you would like to see?

Trusting yourself in business

One of the biggest lessons for me was learning to trust myself in my business. As well as doing courses on online business, I had worked with many small businesses and entrepreneurs and seen how they all did it, so initially, I thought that's how it had to be done.

When you are starting out it's perfect to follow others and do it as others do so that you learn and importantly just begin, but over time, and particularly for entrepreneurs, it's important to find your way and learn to trust yourself and what works for you. After all, for many, one of the main reasons to begin working for yourself is to have the balance you would like. To get to do more of the things you want to do. To work on the things you want to.

It is a process of un-learning in some ways, as we are taught that business needs to be done a certain way, generally adopting a very masculine approach. Absolutely, there is also a need to make money and support yourself, so it can be a fine balance getting that right. Learning to trust yourself and what works for you and your business and life can be a big step for many, and one that evolves over time. Yes, there can be support in having consistency or a plan to work with and from, but where does it come from? Does it come from a place of thinking things have to be done a certain way, or is it fully aligned with you?

What was life-changing for me was beginning to know and trust my intuition in my business and letting it guide me. This was something I came to realise by myself, not from any courses or formal learning I'd undertaken.

As I learned how powerful my intuition is and started to listen to it and check in with it, asking it questions whenever I needed the answer to a decision, I realised the power we all hold inside ourselves. What makes the difference, I feel, is trusting it and following its guidance, not ignoring it or only half-heartedly following what it says.

My intuition has always been right. It is often not the fastest answer I want, but as I look back and connect the dots, I can clearly see how it has always supported me and led me on my perfect path.

At one point, I was pushing to try and make something happen in my corporate wellness business: I had a programme I had sold before and thought I could go down that path and help others there. This was an area I used to be passionate about but wasn't feeling connected to anymore – partly as I no longer worked in that environment and also because I didn't want to go into offices. The only glimmer I had from my intuition was that I needed to work with people in business, but aside from that, it was telling me to wait and be still. Something was coming and bubbling away inside of me. I could literally feel and see it cocooning inside when I did visualisation journeys.

I was working part-time and had a roof over my head, yet I still insisted on trying to make something happen as I thought I should be making more money and sharing this programme. I spent money on it and shared it a few times, but it just wasn't landing or feeling good in my body. There was so much resistance. It was completely wrong for me, and it actually emerged a few months later that it was no longer an area for me to be focusing on.

In fact, in less than an hour, one afternoon in January 2020, I got the whole download for the Empathpreneurs®, working with empath entrepreneurs to support them in the different areas of an online business, which can align to their chakras. And even better, it combined all of my different experiences from my wellness business and the part-time work I had been doing for years.

It was quite a magical moment for me.

It was still working with people in business as I had felt a few months back, but it was for where I was at – with the people I mainly spoke to and worked with. I was quite blown away. I was also leaving my home in London in February 2020 to go back home to Kenya for a bit. Then Covid-19 hit and the world changed, and I couldn't get back to London, so being able to work with empaths in and on their online businesses was perfect for me.

That experience was quite profound and really affirmed the power of trusting your intuition for me, so I have sworn to completely trust every bit of guidance I am given. One of which was to write this book, only four months in! I have a plan for the next few months, which has been totally comforting for my mind, but also, I am not worried about what's next. I check in regularly with my intuition and now know I can chill out a bit more if it goes a bit quiet.

Trust the guidance

Trust the guidance you get from your Higher Self, your intuition, the Universe (or whatever you would like to call it).

It has never let me down. Ever. Things might take longer than you expect, and you most certainly will be led on a path that you can't even imagine, but if you surrender to it, you will be led on the most exciting, magical, interesting, deeply satisfying journey ever.

- Where have you not been listening to or following your guidance?

- How can you begin to trust it more?

Inability to focus and make decisions in your business

This area can link to other chakras, as an inability to make decisions might be due to feeling fearful, stuck or confused, or not having your heart in what you are doing. It is included in this chakra as I have seen it in most clients tie into not having a clear vision for your business and where you are going with it.

It is wonderful working intuitively and allowing what wants to come through in the moment, and I fully recommend leaning into and using this magic. But there is also the grounding of your business with the practical and knowing where you would like to go in it – or at least how you want to feel in it. This will support you with knowing whether opportunities or potential clients who come your way are aligned with you and your business. It will support you with knowing how and where you want to show up. And what activities you can do in your marketing to help you get there.

Not having a clear vision can sometimes lead to indecision as you aren't sure where to focus your energies, or conversely, you say yes to everything that comes your way, leading to a scattered approach that may burn you out.

- Do you have a vision for your business?
- How do you want to feel in your business?
- How can you support yourself to know if a decision is not aligned?

Owning all of your 'spiritual' gifts

Do you own all of your spiritual gifts as an empathpreneur? All of your magic, wisdom, intuitive or perhaps natural healing abilities? For far too long, these gifts have been put to one side – brushed away or seen as 'woo woo' and not real.

Perhaps you are able to channel Divine messages, maybe you have psychic and intuitive capabilities, or you could be a gifted healer who can move energy and see blockages. Whatever you are capable of, you know it deep inside yourself.

I remember when I first met other empathpreneurs who were claiming their spiritual gifts, things like being able to channel, read intuitive messages or create energy systems for clearing and releasing. I was in awe and knew I wanted to do that too.

I knew how strong my intuition was for myself and I wanted to be able to use it to support others. But I was newer to the journey, and most of my friends and family at that time were not spiritual. I felt so much fear about bringing these sorts of things into my work, so I kept it hidden, except for in the occasional one-to-one sessions with clients.

Over time, as I began to work even more intuitively, I felt such an urge to share more about it and knew I had to start claiming it. So I did, little by little. It felt so liberating to do this and I began to attract people who wanted this kind of support. This began to bring the two sides of my life together, so I started to align more, and it was much more fun for me too! There's still more for me to claim and I am working on it as I evolve and grow in my business.

- How about you? Are you claiming your spiritual gifts? Or are you holding them back and pretending they don't exist?
- How can you begin to bring these gifts into the work you do, if that is calling you?

The world needs these gifts and now is the time to start owning them for yourself. Trust that the right people will be attracted to your work as you begin to share and use your spiritual gifts.

Surrender to what is

Surrender to what is, let yourself be carried by the waves.
So often we try to push and 'make' things happen.
But there is so much flow and magic in the surrendering, allowing and trusting.
Know that when the time is right you will be guided and supported to take the action you need.
Let yourself lean into this and trust your path, not someone else's.

#ChakraMessages

Crown Chakra (Sahasrara)

Crown chakra (Sahasrara)

The crown chakra, at the top of the head and skull, is traditionally associated with the colour violet and is connected to higher states of consciousness and a remembrance that we are all part of a greater whole.

Some of the blocks that can come up in the crown chakra that might affect how you show up in business are:

- An inability to see the bigger picture
- Getting stuck in the small things
- Inability to concentrate or focus
- Letting the inner critic take over
- Fears coming up which prevent you from taking aligned action

In this section, there are some stories, tips, and tools to inspire and support you. You might like to pick one at random or work through one a day, week, or month, depending on what you need most right now. Do whatever works for you.

Before that, I invite you to connect with your crown chakra by closing your eyes or lowering your gaze if that feels more comfortable to you. Imagine a ball of purple light just above the top of your head. Imagine it swirling. Imagine it getting brighter and bigger with each breath that you take in.

Are you able to connect with it and visualise it?

What do you feel?

What comes up when you connect to it? If nothing does, that's fine too.

Your purpose is to be as 'you' as you possibly can.
You are held, supported and divinely guided always.

#CrownChakraMessages

What might be stopping you from taking action?

This can come up again and again in your business, for different reasons. Before I began my business I was talking about it for a loooong time before I actually did anything. Ultimately, I was scared to begin. There was fear of failure. Fear of getting it wrong. Fear of being seen. Fear of being judged. Fear of putting myself out there. Fear of having my life change. Basically, a whole lot of fear. The longer I didn't do anything, the longer I wouldn't have to face any of that fear or give it the chance to be real.

The same happened with writing my first book and launching my first programme. The fear of doing it was greater than the fear of not doing it. This kept me in a state of inaction until I worked through some of the fears and the pull to do it became greater.

As my business progressed and I got much better at facing and feeling the fear and taking action, I came up against inaction, resistance, and procrastination in different ways.

This, I realised, could be because of a number of things. Sometimes I would come up against my old procrastinating ways when I was actually trying to do something that wasn't aligned for me or that I didn't really want to do. I learned this the hard way and did push through: doing things I thought I 'should' be doing. I spent money on marketing and design support and then realised I didn't actually want to be doing the programme I had been 'pushing' and spending that money on.

I also find I come up against resistance and don't take action when there is a need for a deeper level of understanding in myself, or when there is something there for me to heal. An example of this is the resistance I met whilst writing my first book. I came up against it a lot as I had to dive into some of my more traumatic experiences and memories in order to write them as a part of my journey. Ultimately, I had to feel a lot and re-live some of the experiences, even feeling them for the first time, as I had spent so much time numbing and shoving down my feelings. So the resistance to this was there. I had to allow myself to go there in a gentle way that, yes, sometimes included inaction, but was actually a powerful time in the overall process.

I also find I come up against resistance and procrastination when I am being called to share even more deeply and visibly. Again, the process allows me to adjust and take it slowly, so that when I do eventually do what I am being called to, I feel that my whole being – or at least the body and mind (my soul is already there) – have adjusted more.

All in all, I've learned to trust that things are perfect. I've learned to look beneath the inaction and see what is really causing it. Here are a few prompts which might support you if and when you come up against inaction, procrastination, or resistance to taking action.

- What are you putting off doing?
- What is coming up for you? What are you feeling?
- What are you afraid of happening if you do take this action?
- What are you afraid of happening if you don't?
- Is it something you really want to do? Why?
- What do you need to support you and how can you give it to yourself?
- Do you still want to take the action now?

Connecting with the field and energy of your business

Learning that every business has a field, and that every service and offering also has a field, was one of the most magical moments I have had in my business and one that continues to serve me on multiple levels.

Grounding yourself first, then setting the intention to tune into the individual field and surrender to it, is like connecting to the essence, guide, CEO and expert of that particular thing.

As you connect with it and get to know it, you feel the energy of the offer or business, you can receive guidance on what action steps to take, you can feel who the audience is, and you will be guided on when to rest and when to move forward. There are no limits to what you can ask about, ask for, and ask to receive, to support you to take the most aligned action.

It can help you when you are blocked or falling into patterns of over-doing and trying to force something to happen. Having this strong connection is such a reassurance for our minds and one of the biggest support systems I have ever received.

Some ways to help you regularly connect to your business, so that you can tap into that support when you need it are:

- Keeping your energy clear. This can include regular movement, letting the energy flow through you, and eating fresh foods.

- Grounding and connecting to the earth in ways that are accessible to you, so that you aren't carrying excess or other's energy.

- Spending time connecting to your intuition. Just like a muscle, this needs to be done regularly to build up that strength.

If you would like a free guided visualisation to help you connect to the energy and field of your business, you can find one in the resources section at the end. This will help you to strengthen your connection with the energy and field of your business, come to it to guide you whenever you need, and ultimately help you move forward with clarity.

Creating energetic containers

Whilst connecting to the field and energy of your business and offerings is truly incredible, creating and being a part of an energetic container with others is even more powerful in terms of bringing things into the physical, and something I have used to birth new creations.

By 'energetic container' I mean being in a space or group with others with the same mission, such as a mastermind, a group training, a circle, or any form of container that is supportive, held and has you working towards something. There is something so potent and alchemical about these spaces; they can support you in any area of your life you choose. Even if it is not specifically related to what you are doing in that group you can use the energy of the space to support and hold you.

I realised this when I was part of a book writing mastermind for my first book: I got my first draft written the day before the mastermind ended. I was in an abundance mastermind and women's circle which I used to help me complete the book, finishing both groups and the book in the same week.

Being in my Colour Mirrors training space helped me to finish the first draft of this Embodied Business book.

I personally used these containers to inspire momentum and completion. But it doesn't have to be for these sorts of projects, it could be for personal healing and growth, or to make a change in your life. Whatever you need, leaning into these spaces can be an added support.

As I've said before, you really don't have to do this journey alone, there is so much magic and support out there for you to tune into.

How your purpose affects your energy levels

Being an empathpreneur can certainly come with its challenges when it comes to your energy levels. This is an area that has felt all over the place, and evolved for me, on my entrepreneurial journey.

It is absolutely linked to basic self-care such as what I eat and drink, the amount of movement I do, time in nature, how much I sleep, and how much time I spend on my laptop or other screens.

But actually, the biggest thing that has emerged is that the more aligned I become with my purpose, the more grounded and embodied I feel, and the more energy I have to show up in all areas of my life.

Purpose is a big area, and I do feel that we can have a few purposes in life. For example, I know that expressing myself through art is one of mine: my whole world literally changes and I connect to the flow of the Universe when I am in that space of creation.

I feel that joy and connecting to others on a truly deep, heartfelt level is a part of our purpose as humans and doing this is completely energising and soul-filling. I know a part of my purpose is to give back and help in a few key ways during my time on Earth – for me in particular, helping the environment, and orphans and unwanted children. When I am able to contribute financially to these causes I believe in, or give my time and love, I know how overflowing with energy and love I feel.

But I want to share more here about purpose when it comes to your work and how you are being called to serve through your business, as an empathpreneur.

For me, this has been a gradual journey, and one I know that is still evolving as I find myself refining and homing in on what I am being called to do and how I am being called to show up.

Two factors that have been integral here are trust and patience. From day one I wanted to have everything sorted out straight away, to be serving everyone I was here to work with, and to have it all figured out. But allowing your unique journey to unfold is such a huge part of the process. Trialling the things that don't work and those that do, and learning from it all, leads to you ultimately growing and evolving and truly connecting with your highest purpose.

I have gone through many different areas of focus in my own business. I began with wellbeing in the workplace, then moved to focus entirely on self-care – which narrowed down into seasonal and cyclical self-care. Then my focus was the spiritual side of our lives and this led into embodiment and connecting with our beings. All while I was working part-time as a virtual assistant (VA) and in PR, marketing and business support.

As you can see it hasn't been a straight line. It has been messy, ungrounded and just bloody hard at times. Especially in the early days as I was finding my way and trying out things. There were times when I wanted to quit as I wasn't attracting clients or making any money from my business. I felt like a busy unemployed person (as one of my dear friends who was also self-employed so eloquently described), and I was exhausted a lot of the time.

But each part of my entrepreneurial journey so far has been important for me in some way, even if not what I initially expected, and I know will continue to be. Each part has supported me in some way that has been for my growth and led me closer to my purpose. As I've experimented, trialled and refined, I've noticed my energy levels changing. I learned how tired I would feel holding space for things that didn't fill me up: my energy felt depleted when I started something, such as an offering, that wasn't really for me, but was instead something I thought I should be doing; and I would need even more decompression time after work that I found uninspiring or not in my zone of genius.

As I have moved closer and closer to my purpose my work is more inspiring, fulfilling, stimulating and challenging – all at the same time – and makes me feel like I am making a difference. As I become more aligned with my purpose, I feel it deep within my being and I connect with that magical flow state filled with boundless energy.

- How connected to your purpose do you feel right now, and how does this affect your energy levels and how you are able to show up?
- Are there any areas in your business that are draining you as they aren't in alignment with your purpose? What can you do to change this?

Fears and blocks around technology

Another fear that might stop you from taking the aligned action you need to in your business is a fear of technology, which is actually a mask for a deeper issue.

Yes, technology might not come so easily to some, particularly if you aren't a millennial and didn't grow up with a mobile phone glued to your hand. It can also be easy to feel overwhelmed by it and feel the fatigue caused by a lot of time spent on it.

But, ultimately, technology is a tool to help us, particularly if you are an empathpreneur with an online business (which I'm guessing you are, as you are reading this book). It is a gift of the Aquarian age and something that will support you in reaching the people you are here to work with, create the change you are here to make, and have the impact you desire.

The sooner you embrace that the sooner you will get to what's really going on, if technology is a block for you.

One of my dear older clients who didn't have a mobile phone until her late-thirties is a wonderful example of someone who feared tech. She was totally resistant to using Zoom for our first call. She told me that she had made loads of excuses and was going to let it stop her from making that first call with me. She later admitted that she had so much fear around facing up to the need to make changes and knew she was using her tech fear as an excuse not to show up for herself. She did though, and today, having worked through so much, she even supports and encourages other women in her community to embrace the power and gift of technology in their lives.

Getting fatigued by technology, with all the updates and changes happening all the time, as well as the very nature of it, can be a block sometimes too, but if you are feeling constantly exhausted by technology, it's a sign to take a break!

- How do you feel about using technology?
- What is stopping you from fully embracing it in your business?
- What might you really be holding onto here?

The power of vibration

I want to share a story with you to illustrate how powerfully you can change your outside world when you change your inner world. This is not a business story, but the effects of it have rippled out into all areas of my life, and at the time of writing this, I am still seeing shifts and changes happen.

Many of my deep inner shifts and transformations happened on a whole new level when I started working with colour and tuning into, and healing, my ancestral and past life memories. Much of this work happened for me during lockdown, when I got 'stuck' in Kenya, alone with my youngest brother (and his wonderful carers) who has many special needs. My brother is blind, has brain damage, and has cerebral palsy, amongst other things. I love him dearly and he is one of the most beautiful souls and cheekiest, funniest people I know, but he is also challenging as his needs are unique and he can demand a lot of attention.

I felt quite overwhelmed in the early days of being with him, as I felt all the responsibility of being there with him without our parents (they were stuck in France). I had only planned to be back in Kenya for a couple of months and then go back to the UK, but this now changed everything. I was also used to being more in control of my own time, but now had to be with him every afternoon for a bit and then in the evenings – which wasn't so easy as I am much more of a morning person – with no end in sight.

As the reality of the situation sunk in, I found it really hard. I hate to admit it, but I would resent most of the evenings and couldn't wait to get into bed when I would have peace and quiet and be on my own. I found my brother really loud and I felt so angry and definitely went into victim mode about being there in that situation.

But, as I began to go deeper into the anger, the sadness, the victimhood, and other things I was feeling, old stories and memories from my childhood were brought up. Things I hadn't dealt with from that time began to re-surface. Stories about responsibility and feeling like I always had to be the one to look after my siblings in difficult situations. Feeling like my parents always got out of being the responsible ones. As these things began to come up, I was able to heal and transform them through taking back my power and owning myself as an adult.

As I did this, I began to notice a huge difference in my brother. He would be quieter and gentler in the evenings, and I found myself really beginning to enjoy being with him again. As I continued on my deep diving and shifting my emotions and triggers that were coming up, completely changing my vibration and how I felt internally, he kept on mirroring it back.

One of the biggest changes I saw was after working through and releasing a deep-held trauma in my sacral chakra. I came into the room to be with him, feeling lighter but emotionally exhausted and expecting to have to give him attention. Instead, he asked me for a big hug, which he only did before when he wanted something, and kept asking for them all afternoon. It was so heart-warming and such an affirmation of my energy shifts happening inside, being mirrored by my brother who could only feel the energy of what had been happening.

After that, I also began to get more enquiries on my website and booked in more discovery calls than I had ever previously booked in one week.

- Are you aware of how your vibration affects you day-to-day?
- What areas are you being called to look at in your life, and what changes could you make, to support you with attracting what you desire?

Working with your inner critic

We all have an inner critic. A voice inside ourselves that can be louder or quieter depending on what's happening. A voice that tells us not to do something new. Not to put ourselves out there. Not to take action on something that might feel scary.

This voice may have come from childhood when you were told not to act a certain way; it could be from a parent who was fearful and stopped you trying new things; it may be from a movie or something you read which influenced you to not want to feel a certain way and to stop yourself if ever those feelings arose.

If you have a particularly strong inner critic at a certain time or in a certain situation you might want to get to the bottom of where this voice comes from, either with support or alone, and then re-write it to a new empowering belief, or shift it with EFT, NLP or another modality.

I also want to suggest taking action as one of the most powerful ways to work with and quieten that inner critic.

It's feeling the fear and hearing the voice and still showing up. Taking the little steps that you know are for you. Feeling uncomfortable as you do it. Re-writing your path right now and not letting the voice of your inner critic control you.

- What action can you take in an area where your inner critic has been the one in charge?

Creating a business that is in alignment

For too long we have worked in a world that puts profits over wellness and leaves people feeling burned out, overwhelmed, stressed and suffering from a number of health conditions.

I know many people go into business to create more time and freedom for themselves, to feel more nourished by getting to spend time with the people they love, to travel, and to be able to enjoy this planet and all it has to offer. But often these same people get pulled into working all hours and at any cost.

I do believe there is a balance that can be achieved here that is unique to you as an individual, and can be achieved by checking in regularly with yourself to see how you feel and where you are at. However, there's also something else that has helped me – you may already be familiar with it but I have slightly adapted it.

What's helped me is having key feelings and qualities for each area of my business in alignment with my chakras, for me to refer to as an indicator of whether something nourishes me and is worth putting my energy into.

I use the chakras to represent the different parts of my business – as mentioned in the introduction – as well as my wellbeing in that area.

Base chakra – business basics, systems and processes
Grounded
Boundaried
Rested

Sacral chakra – branding and identity
Flowing
Creative
Held

Solar plexus chakra – wellbeing and self-care
Embodied
Joyful
Nourished

Heart chakra – any sharing and marketing materials
Connected
Loving
Authentic

Throat chakra – communication and expression
Clear
Purposeful
True

Third eye chakra – vision and planning
Intuitive
Magical
Present

Crown chakra – alignment with purpose
Peaceful
Aligned
Spacious

These feelings can be a benchmark for whether or not to say 'yes' to something, or for little check-ins when it comes to how you feel.

- How does this resonate for you?
- What are your key feelings or values that you might like to support you with aligning each chakra in your business?

Soul Star Chakra (Vyapini)

Soul star chakra (Vyapini)

In this section you will find some suggestions for connecting to the Divine Love that is available to you and that you ultimately are.

The Divine Love of the soul star

The soul star is the portal to Divine Love.

It is the holding and embrace that comes from the Divine.

It is the anchor reminding you that you, too, are Divine Love, your body is Divine Love, all aspects of you are Divine Love. Everything in your life – all of your experiences – has been perfect and an expression of that love. They may not have all felt good, or been easy, but they have all been for you. To help you remember love by experiencing both it and its opposite.

You are here to anchor that Divine Love on earth and to be one of the many who are here to bring about the new earth. Heaven has always been inside of you and you can anchor it on earth by being you. The most you that you can possibly be. Loving, welcoming and shining a light on all parts of you, as they are all Divine.

Whenever you feel unsure or that it's too much, surrender to the love of the Divine. Connect to it and remember the truth of who you are: a Divine being here to experience life in physical form, in all of its expressions.

Let go and let love lead, trusting that you are on the right path, it's all unfolding as it should, and you are so held and supported.

You are Divine Love.

Remembering that everything is happening for you

The entrepreneurial journey can be hard!

You might feel like you aren't getting there – wherever 'there' is.
You might feel like you aren't enough.
You might have times with many different jobs, wondering if they'll ever end.
You might have to ditch parts of your business as you evolve and refine.
You might have times with no work.
You might have times with too much work.
You might have times when you work with clients who are looking to be rescued.
You might have times with clients that don't want to pay.
You might feel overwhelmed and exhausted by it all.
You might wonder what you are doing and where you are going.
You might think it's too hard and that you aren't meant to be doing it.

But I want to share a little reminder and invitation to look at your journey, with its complete range of experiences and demands, and know that it is all perfect. It is all happening as it is meant to. You will gain something from each experience, even if you don't realise it at the time. Sometimes it could be a new skill, other times it may be a little bit more confidence or belief in yourself. It could be to see and learn how others do it. To meet and experience new people and make connections. To learn what works and what doesn't work. Or perhaps to shed layers that you are holding onto, to support your own growth and expansion.

You are always exactly where you need to be. You have always been, and will continue to be, given exactly what you can handle at the time. It is all happening for you.

- How can you begin to look at your journey so far with the remembering and knowing that it has all happened for you? (And keep remembering to do this as you go onward?)

Compassion for all parts of yourself

How can you give more compassion and understanding to all parts of yourself?

Especially the parts that don't feel so good or that you perhaps 'judge'.

Maybe it's the part of you that is anxious and frustrated?

Or perhaps the part that feels lost and confused?

The part that isn't 'keeping it together' and that just wants to give up?

What would you say to someone else feeling the things you are feeling?

Vibrational alignment

When it comes to having a business that nourishes you, feeling good vibrationally is fundamental as you will do the best work and be the most you. Of course, we all have days or even weeks that don't feel so good, but it's up to you to support yourself to bring yourself back into alignment, so that those times don't stop you from showing up as you are here to do.

The more vibrationally aligned you feel, the more you will be supported by the Divine and the more you will be able to give and show up. So I truly recommend prioritising this and doing what it takes to support yourself. Notice the days when you don't feel so good, and what might have caused this. Make changes, adjust and refine as you go.

Rather than give you a list of all the practices you could do, I've listed a few categories to feel into and questions to ask yourself.

- Physical wellbeing
- Mental wellbeing
- Emotional wellbeing
- Nourishment (all food and drink you are consuming)
- Creativity
- Energy levels
- Sleep and rest

- How do these areas look in your life right now in terms of your self-care? For this you could write down what you are doing to support yourself and perhaps rate how you feel about it in your life.

- What more could you do to support yourself in each area?

Then it's up to you to make time in your schedule to look after yourself in these areas. I recommend making small changes in only one or two areas to begin, then adding others as these changes become more ingrained.

If this is an area you would like more support with, please take a look in the resources section at the end for some ways I can help.

What do you have that's just for you?

What do you have in your life that's just for you?
Not for your business or your clients.
Not for anyone else, just for you.
Something that support you and fills you up on a deep level.
Something that shows yourself you are worth your love and attention.
This is so important for your wellbeing in many ways.
But most of all, you're affirming you are worthy and giving to yourself.

APPENDIX

Chakra wellness overview

Whilst this is a book to support you in business, it would be remiss of me not to mention the importance of wellness and share some practices to support you holistically with each of the seven main chakras. We are interconnected beings and I really want to emphasise the importance of this when looking at your business. I feel the current way of working in the western world, although changing, has led very much to compartmentalising the different areas of our lives and pushing through as though we are machines. This has led to multiple health issues – mentally, physically, emotionally, and spiritually.

Some of the issues absolutely overlap and you might experience issues in a few chakras. If you are ever not sure which chakra you need support with, I recommend looking at the bigger picture of what's going on in your life, always intuitively trusting yourself, and you will gain awareness into which chakra you need and/or want to work on.

As an empathpreneur you likely are already aware of this and have practices that support you. But in this section, you will find some of the more common issues that might come up for empathpreneurs and how they can link to each chakra, along with a few different practices and tools that will holistically support the wellness of that chakra. Please note that even though an issue is listed for a specific chakra, it doesn't mean it can't come up in others. These just tend to be the ones they correspond to.

This list is not exhaustive by any means; I haven't included much detail on things like yoga and pranayama which are both wonderful practices for connecting to and working with your chakras. If you are interested in going deeper in any area there are many wonderful teachers, authors and practitioners who will be able to guide you further. I also always recommend reaching out if you need any support.

Base chakra (Muladhara)

Issues that relate to it: adrenal fatigue, anger, anxiety, lower back pain, some digestive issues, fear, shame, weight issues, stress

Colour: red

Foods: pomegranate, cherries, grapes, plums, beans, tomatoes, raspberries, strawberries, peppers, and foods that are grown in the earth

Crystals: haematite, garnet, ruby, red jasper, obsidian

Essential oils to use: patchouli, cedarwood, basil, sandalwood, frankincense

Wellness practices:

- Grounding practices such as getting out into nature and lying on the ground.
- Have red things around you, paint with red colours, wear red. Colour can really affect us, and although red might seem like a colour that instils anger, it actually has been proven to induce a grounded, calm feeling.
- Dance barefoot, move your body intuitively, connect to your sensuality.
- De-clutter and get rid of items you don't need.
- Chant the mantra sound corresponding to this chakra: "LAM."

Sacral chakra (Svadhisthana)

Issues that relate to it: adrenal fatigue, anxiety, lower back pain, some digestive issues, guilt, shame, trauma, abuse, stress, weight issues, co-dependency

Colour: orange

Foods: pumpkin, sweet potatoes, mangoes, orange melon, oranges, squash, papaya, apricots, orange lentils

Crystals: carnelian, orange calcite, peach moonstone (I also like rose quartz as this is considered a feminine chakra)

Essential oils to use: neroli, bergamot, orange, cinnamon, ylang ylang

Wellness practices:

- Allow yourself to feel your feelings.
- Do things that feel like play.
- Spend time in or near water, as the element for this chakra is water.

- Dance – especially dancing that really encourages movement in that area, such as belly dancing.
- Practice hula-hooping.
- Learn Tantra to get in touch with your sexuality on a more conscious level.
- Connect with your creativity in a way that works for you, using it as a way to channel your emotions.
- Wear and have the colour orange around you.
- Chant the mantra sound corresponding to this chakra: "VAM."

Solar plexus chakra (Manipura)

Issues that relate to it: addictions, eating disorders, anxiety, middle back pain, some digestive issues, fear, guilt, panic attacks, stress, weight issues, self-esteem or confidence issues

Colour: yellow

Foods: corn, lemons, bananas, pineapple, grapefruit, starfruit, yellow lentils, yellow peppers, chamomile

Crystals: tiger's eye, citrine, topaz, yellow jade, amber

Essential oils to use: grapefruit, lemon, juniper berry, black pepper, lemongrass, coriander

Wellness practices:

- Connect with the element of fire.
- Get into the sunshine.
- Wear and have the colour yellow or gold around you.
- Do core-strengthening practices and twists.
- Chant the mantra sound corresponding to this chakra: "RAM."

Heart chakra (Anahata)

Issues that relate to it: anxiety, upper or middle back pain, loneliness, depression, disconnection

Colour: green

Foods: green vegetables – particularly leafy ones, matcha, spirulina, green apples, dandelion greens, herbs such as parsley and coriander, kiwi fruit, limes, avocados, cacao, raw/good quality dark chocolate

Crystals: malachite, green jade, rose quartz, aventurine

Essential oils to use: rose, eucalyptus, ylang ylang, geranium, lavender

Wellness practices:
- Practice regular self-care and self-love, and loving kindness (metta meditation).
- Practice Ho'oponopono – 'Thank you, forgive me, I'm sorry, I love you'.
- Wear and have the colours green or pink around you.
- Watch or read romantic movies/stories.
- Connect with the element of air.
- Do heart opening stretches – around your chest and back area.
- Chant the mantra sound corresponding to this chakra: "YAM."

Throat chakra (Vishudda)

Issues that relate to it: anxiety, upper back pain, neck pain, self-expression
Colour: blue
Foods: blueberries, blackberries, spirulina, foods and drinks that are soothing on the throat such as herbal teas, syrups made from elderberries or elderflowers, eucalyptus, sage, liquorice
Crystals: blue lace agate, turquoise, lapis lazuli, blue tiger's eye
Essential oils to use: basil, peppermint, spearmint, chamomile, tea tree
Wellness practices:
- Sing, chant or speak up.
- Drink warm tea to soothe your throat.
- Wear and have the colour blue around you.
- Spend more time listening to others.
- Listen to music.
- Chant the mantra sound corresponding to this chakra: "HAM."

Third eye chakra (Ajna)

Issues that relate to it: anxiety, headaches, issues relating to eyes, ears or nose, worry, irritability
Colour: indigo
Foods: blueberries, blackberries, blackcurrants, pineapple (as it is good for the pineal gland in the third eye)
Crystals: lapis lazuli, sapphire, amethyst, sodalite
Essential oils to use: clary sage, frankincense, rosemary, sandalwood, lavender, vetiver

Wellness practices:
- Spend time remembering and connecting to your dreams. Keep a dream journal.
- Spend time looking at the moon and stars.
- Wear and have the colour indigo around you.
- Practice balancing yoga postures.
- Chant the mantra sound corresponding to this chakra: "OM or AUM."

Crown chakra (Sahasrara)

Issues that relate to it: anxiety, depression, fatigue, headaches, sleep issues, moodiness

Colour: violet/purple

Foods: purple cabbage, purple grapes, purple peppers, purple carrots, eggplant, berries, purple asparagus, plums, also fasting and detoxing

Crystals: clear quartz, amethyst, diamond, moonstone, selenite, fluorite, labradorite

Essential oils to use: rosemary, sandalwood, frankincense, myrrh, lavender, cedarwood

Wellness practices:
- Learn something new.
- Spend time meditating.
- Wear and have the colour violet/purple around you.
- Practice inversions like handstands or headstands.
- Practice gratitude.
- Chant the mantra sound corresponding to this chakra: "OM or AUM"

Next steps

If you are looking for support in your business – with either any blocks that might be coming up or the practical side of things – I invite you to book a free breakthrough session with me to get to know one another and feel into what it might be like to work together.

You can book a session and have a look at the other ways I can support you on my website:

www.empathpreneurs.org.

Embodied Business Resources

http://empathpreneurs.org/resources - on this page you can access links for all of these things and more as they get added:

- A visualisation to connect to Mother Earth.
- A regression meditation.
- A visualisation to connect to the energy and field of your business.
- A template for tracking your seasons and cycles to support you in your business.
- My free community on Facebook: Empathpreneurs – Creating a business that nourishes you.
- My first book: Embodied – A self-care guide for sensitive souls.
- A journey through the chakras – a wellbeing course with modules containing visualisations, prompts, tools and practices to support you with wellness specific to each chakra.
- The e-book from the community project 'My sensitivity is a strength', combining stories, insights, and inspiration on what it's like being a sensitive person in business, from a number of different contributors.

Author bio

I have 20 years of varied experience working in and with businesses, ranging from global corporations and brands, to soulpreneurs and hospitality entrepreneurs. I have worked full-time, part-time and freelance in many different roles, from PR and marketing, to HR, business operations and as a PA/VA.

I am the author of Embodied – A self-care guide for sensitive souls, which was published in July 2019, a Colour Mirrors practitioner, and holistic health and wellness coach supporting empathpreneurs with their wellbeing, particularly in today's fast-paced world.

I support empathpreneurs with all areas of their business – from the practical side of systems and processes, planning, marketing and PR (done in a way to support sensitive souls), to the inner work of limiting beliefs and blocks – through colour therapy, past-life and ancestral regressions and inner child work.

Wellness is an essential part of the work I do. No more burn out and hustling at all hours – which is simply NOT sustainable. Wellness is integral to enable you to create a business that nourishes you and supports the planet.

Acknowledgments

Thank you to all those who have paved the way and been such an inspiration for me, in particular Rachel – I am so grateful for all I have learned from you, for believing in me and for re-igniting my entrepreneur spark as an adult.

The hugest thank you to my wonderful entrepreneur and empathpreneur friends of whom I am blessed to have many today.

Thank you so much my dear Meron for reading an early draft of this book and giving me such helpful feedback. I am so lucky to have you in my life.

The hugest thank you to the early reviewers: Vix, Nicola, Julia, Anna, Lulu, Sarah, Meron and Ngosa – I am so, so grateful to you all for your time and energy and am so honoured to receive your heartfelt reviews.

Thank you Katherine for holding such a powerful, life-changing space for my Colour Mirrors training. It has been one of the greatest blessings of my life so far.

Shannon, I am truly blessed to have met you and work with you. You have shown me the absolute joy of working with another empath, honouring the feminine (and masculine), trusting the timing, plus so much more. Thank you.

Thank you so much to all of my clients, I am so honoured I get to support you on your journeys, it is a privilege to do this work with you and I thank you for all that you each have taught me.

To all the members in my Facebook group, Empathpreneurs – Creating a business that nourishes you, thank you for being a part of my community. I am so grateful to you all for being in this space with me and allowing me to share.

Thank you David, Maya and Lele for being my biggest fans and supporters on my entrepreneurial journey from day one! Thank you also to the rest of my family for being so supportive and encouraging me on this path, I'm grateful for you all.

Thank you Nolly and Mary for looking after me, and being all around amazing whilst I wrote this book in the short amount of time it wanted to be written in.

Thank you dad for making all of this possible and for always believing in me. I am so lucky to have you.

Last but not least, Nicola, Anna, and Lynda – thank you for all your help getting this book ready. Thank you especially Nicola for this space to create and share. It is such an honour to be a part of the UNBOUND family.